Seeds of Tomorrow

To Dov —
Thank you for leading
the way!
In spirited partnership,
Andy Paul

Seeds of Tomorrow

Solutions for Improving Our Children's Education

Angela Engel

Foreword by Deborah Meier

Paradigm Publishers

Boulder • London

Published in the United States by Paradigm Publishers, 3360 Mitchell Lane Suite E, Boulder, CO 80301 USA.

Paradigm Publishers is the trade name of Birkenkamp & Company, LLC, Dean Birkenkamp, President and Publisher.

Library of Congress Cataloging-in-Publication Data
Engel, Angela.
Seeds of tomorrow : solutions for improving our children's education / by Angela Engel ; forword by Deborah Meier.
p. cm.
Includes bibliographical references and index.
ISBN 978-1-59451-778-5 (hardcover : alk. paper)
1. School improvement programs—United States. I. Title.
II. Title: Solutions for educating America's children.
LB2822.82.E545 2010
371.2'07—dc22
2009025507

Printed and bound in the United States of America on acid-free paper that meets the standards of the American National Standard for Permanence of Paper for Printed Library Materials.

DESIGNED AND TYPESET BY JANE RAESE

09 10 11 12 13 ∽ 5 4 3 2 1

Dedicated to the memory of Dr. Marie Wirsing,

who planted the first seeds,

and to all the world's seedlings—

may you bloom brilliantly.

Contents

Foreword

by Deborah Meier

It's about time someone wrote this book. Probably a lot of what Angela Engel sets forth here has been said before—but never has it been said better, and never in such a straight-forward, reader-friendly, and well-reasoned order.

She starts with the history of standardized testing itself, which might put some readers off, but it is very critical. What standardized testing has served has always been two very opposite purposes—which are both bad because they come down to judging most individuals, as well as for judging "kinds" of people—by race, class, gender, etc. But standardized testing also has highlighted trends and biases of importance—that is bringing good judgment to the results and tolerating the considerable measurement error embedded in the technology of the instruments. Actually, Engel is kind and doesn't dwell on how little these tests can tell us about how and why children give "wrong" answers, or why teaching "for" right answers is so damaging. She spends less time on the issue of narrowing the curriculum than other writers have. But she is crystal clear on what's at stake in using such instruments to produce a modern democracy.

I've always been intrigued with our innocence in the face of thousands of years of assumptions about why some people are "lesser," why the haves are naturally advantaged and the have-nots are naturally disadvantaged. At the nation closest to America's "soul"—England—with a reading of most of its standard literary classics, the story is told over and over: There is something fundamentally inferior about the poor. Even reformer Charles Dickens explained the sensitivity and intelligence of his hero Oliver Twist by his genetic inheritance. Even his standard upper-class language had come to him "biologically."

It is hardly then a surprise that the inventors of our systems of measurement have taken the results of such tests for granted. They would have tossed their researches, had common sense not prevailed—the winners and losers were precisely whom they expected them to be. In fact, that's where researchers started— by comparing questions that winners got right and losers got wrong. The tests were a perfect match, and it was called Science.

It is hard indeed for us overnight to slough off the mindset that blames the victims, that insists that, since it is a meritocratic and individualistically free society, there is no excuse for failure. It's either genetically predetermined (which we're happily not allowed to say), or a personal choice. Given that neither Angela nor I accept the genetic explanation (there are those out there who are ready to pounce on this explanation again), or that it matches the desires of the families or students of color, we're distressed at the idea that the only alternative must be the sheer laziness or racism on the part of schools. We acknowledge some of the latter, but laziness is a word that covers up a whole host of other dilemmas that frequent external testing leaves untouched and, in fact, makes worse.

And then Engel tackles the second story—from the testing industry's low point in the late 1970s, to its current popularity (although it's far more popular among politicians and leading elites than among the public at-large)—the tale of how the promising movement for "standards" got hijacked into a movement for standardization via testing. It was then that a promising and critical moment for a different paradigm of reform was lost. There was a time that I thought "my side" would win— between 1975 and 1990, or thereabouts. The work of Ted Sizer had hit a nerve in American education—too idealistic, perhaps, said critics, but surely right on. Sizer placed no blame, pointed no fingers, but offered a different and sensible path out of a longstanding tension between liberal arts traditionalists and progressive-minded reformers. There can be high standards without standardization and without elitism.

Within a few years, the language of standards became not an aspirational call, a glad waving toward a finer future, but a lockstep system of test preparation, scripted teaching, and incurious students. It deprives schools of their most important constituency—their roots in each and every community's own experiences and wisdom, and their hopes for their young. Accountability may, as in the banking industry, require larger doses of localism than we've grown accustomed to thinking.

Or, as Engel notes in Chapter 3, testing can become a feigned system of accountability—a mystification on such a grand scale that few note the sleight of hand. She lays it out. And she also reminds us of some simple propositions that should direct real accountability. She hints at an uncomfortable truth—someone besides kids, parents, teachers, or even the larger economy may benefit from our misdirection. The quote Engel uncovered from Harold McGraw III stunned me. The testing industry with all its money, prestige, and political connections found a new market that far eclipsed the old one. The politics of President George W. Bush and the new role envisioned for the testing industry were married in a ceremony that produced No Child Left Behind. Disclosure: I'm a board member of the one and only "lobbying" group that concerns itself with testing fairness—FairTest—which operates out of a single room with three to four employees.

Chapter 4 takes us to the challenges we're up against. Engel explores the issue of schooling and the economy, the appeal of privatization, the concept of merit pay, and teacher's unions, and ends with poverty and race. Then, Chapter 4 switches to these questions: Is there a solution? Can we teach them to fish? Engel is optimistic—as I am too—that such answers exist, and she points us in the direction of producing children who can do better than fish for "the right answers," which is the focus of Chapter 6.

Chapter 5 tackles the issue of choice—which is dear to my heart. I was a pioneer for pubic school choice, and like Engel, I still see it as critical to good schooling. But like her, I also see the wisdom of not trying to force everyone's children into the same orientation toward schooling. Engel outlines four reasonable overarching approaches and why the solution must include making choices accessible as fully as possible. The dilemmas that choice offers—charter schools, magnets, or even vouchers—pose different trade-offs. She sees these trade-offs as related to the amount of money we are willing to spend on having a great educational system. Too often, she suggests, the choices are disguises for spending less money on other people's children.

And finally, in Chapter 6, Engel lays out some potential solutions. The answers lie in part in creating a national conversation that teachers, parents, and grandparents participate in—to open up our minds to the possibilities. Such a conversation would require us to explore other acceptable forms of accountability that get closer to what it is we care most about. She's properly impatient with the long conversations within academic circles, the whining of teachers (my word), and a show of sustained protest by those who already know better. The list is long—and includes a wide swatch of the American professional class, as well as its teachers and parents. But it's not at the head of the line at conferences I attend. We even have alternatives ready to go, long used in the best of public and independent schools. (Note that the elite send their kids to schools that rarely use standardized tests and are not covered by NCLB.) We have examples from the international community. What we lack is a sufficient sense of responsibility to do something about it. That's the underlying passion that comes through in this book.

Engel sums it up neatly, and I intend to memorize this: "We will always be negotiating who to become and what kind of world we want to live in. Our Constitution was created not so that government could shape our political, economic, and social system, but so that we the people could."

And then, as Engel does throughout, she goes back to children and classrooms with the wonderful children's story, *Stone Soup*. If we're determined enough we can make soup out of anything. . . .

This is a book filled with teacher and parent stories, but always in clear service of weeding out nineteenth-century notions of sorting and tracking—of who are the leaders and who the followers—that have infused themselves into the twenty-first-century culture of schooling—under new labels and false "scientific" theories. It's also a reminder of what a difference it makes when the storyteller is close to the work to be done. It's time for such experts to be part of the policy-team that has driven us into this dead-end with their infatuation with the mindless manipulation of numbers.

The book doesn't ignore the sometimes bleaker side of the current situation, but it also provides inspiration and optimism about what an informed public can do. The book is an essential part of the toolkit for the reforms that can be undertaken to fulfill the promise of education that has always been flirted with, often practiced here and there, and that could if we follow her wise words, be our future.

Acknowledgments

In the fall of 2003 I entered a master's program at the University of Colorado at Denver. Dr. Marie Wirsing was the professor of my educational philosophy class. In her seventies, her soft tone matched her petite frame and disguised a powerful and enlightened spirit.

At the beginning of our first class, she wrote a single sentence on the white board: "The conditions gave rise to Hitler's Nazi Germany." Throughout that semester we studied four models of philosophy within the context of education and the Holocaust. It was during that time that I began to grasp a deeper understanding of the ideological frameworks and value systems that shape today's policies, attitudes, and societal norms.

The philosophy class was followed with an independent study. Afternoons spent drinking tea at Dr. Wirsing's kitchen table is where the *Seeds of Tomorrow* first germinated. Instead of enrolling in the doctoral program, I began my research. That same fall Dr. Wirsing died quietly in a hospital bed. During the thirty years she was a professor at the University of Colorado at Denver, and even earlier, when she was a history teacher at Englewood High School, she inspired thousands of students. Of course, that is what great teachers do.

In addition, I'd like to express my deepest gratitude to my husband, Paul, who made this book and my work possible. I also thank my daughters, Grace and Sophie, who slept soundly through the late night tap, tap, tappings of the keyboard.

I am grateful for Deborah Meier, who courageously shines the light and graciously clears the path for others to follow, and to Dean Birkenkamp and the Paradigm team who said "yes" to an unknown author during a tenuous trade book market. I am thankful to the many friends and colleagues who provided countless reads and reviews. Particular recognition goes to Dr.

Tod Parker, who tended the book's completion with his frequent reminders, "All you have to do is tell the truth."

To avoid any angry phone calls and letters of dissolution, I want to pay tribute to my mother, Jennifer Cortner. Thank you for living the example of writer and for teaching me what it looks like to stand up in the world. Also to your credit are the occasions where I thought I had written something brilliant only to return later and proclaim, "What was I thinking?"

Thank you to Stuart Brann for the tea and edits. I am especially appreciative of Don Perl and my teachers who carry the lessons of courage and conviction. In times of darkness I have opened my eyes to discover a friendship circle of immense wisdom and beauty—thank you. This journey has taught me that we are all seed carriers. I hope you will consider this book, *Seeds of Tomorrow,* an acknowledgment of you. ·

We pray for the seeds of our future.
Bless our children that they may blossom and
bring beauty to those among them.

Guide us, your gardeners, in cultivating
our fields of tomorrow.

Teach us to shape paths where love and wisdom flow.
Grant us rich ground to support the roots below.

Help us to extract the weeds of hate and indifference
and nourish with understanding and acceptance.

Lead us in teaching them to share in the light so
that each one may grow tall and strong and
none are left in the shade of another.

Bring us the winds of change,
the cleansing rain,
the brilliant sun, and
the promise of new growth.

Prepare our earth for greatness,
your gardeners have been readied and
the new seedlings are awakening
to the first light of a new day.

Introduction

Have you heard the story of stone soup? There are many versions and several cultural variations describing the tale of a village that is deeply divided, overcome with fear and famine. A stranger comes to the village and is greeted with slammed doors and closed curtains. Using a large pot and some stones, the stranger makes a fire and begins making stone soup. The residents remain in hiding, at first watching as the fire beneath the pot grows red hot. The stranger attentively stirs the soup that's just beginning to boil. Soon the observers grow curious and one by one begin to abandon the security of their dwellings. Dipping a ladle into the pot and bringing it to his lips, the stranger whispers to himself, "Mmm, it tastes good, but it may be missing something." A little girl with dirt-stained curls speaks up from the crowd, "I was digging onions in the garden this morning. I will run and get some for the soup." The pot cooks the onions, and again the stranger dips his ladle and brings the broth to his mouth. "Mmm, tastes good, but it may be missing something," he says. A drifter with thread-bare trousers steps out from the shadows and without speaking reaches into a torn pocket for a small bag. His weathered hands reach over the pot, and tiny salt crystals drop and dissolve on the clear surface. Mothers, proprietors, farmers, and grandfathers decide to bring something to add to the pot: cabbage, chicken legs, carrots, potatoes, spices, herbs, and so forth. Before long, they have a delicious soup brewing. As the villagers sit and eat and talk, their hunger is satiated and friendships ripen. The soup warms them, and they learn how coming together and contributing can withstand famine and chase away the darkest of fears.

I begin with this familiar childhood fable because it illustrates the dynamic between the individual and the greater community. This book, seemingly about education, is actually about much more.

While I have written it for a broad audience, some theorists may think that the writing is too impassioned. Teachers and school officials may say that it is too academic. Education analysts may complain that it didn't support their models. This book is not the recipe. It is the stone. Ultimately, what becomes of our children and our schools is answered in what becomes of you individually and all of us collectively.

It is the nature of humanity to test the boundaries of our control and to exercise power by knowing its limitations. The challenge of today's citizenry is mitigating fear and freedom. The freer we become, the greater the uncertainties. As we exercise greater control over society and human beings, we lessen the fear, and we also lesson our freedom. We are constantly negotiating the balance between controlling the outcomes and preserving independence.

Over the centuries, humankind has sought to control nature—the nature of the world, nature of animals, and the nature of men and women. In many cases, humankind has been successful. We have captured wind and sun and rain. We have tamed the beast. We have shaped mountains and eradicated them. We have stopped the rivers and channeled the sea. We have sacrificed, imprisoned, owned, and traded human beings. We have, in countless instances, directed our own future.

It is the elements still beyond our control and the ambiguity of an uncertain tomorrow that compel so many today. Everywhere we see forces working to mechanize, systemize, standardize, and industrialize. The ability to measure and quantify leads us to believe that once calculated we can control the natural variables, even the human ones. The same themes in education are prevalent in health care, environment, economics, and social politics.

The drive to control and manipulate the future has strengthened societies, and it has destroyed them. Ultimately, we as a democratic society must choose between the discomfort of freedom or the safety of constraint.

This isn't just a book about improving our schools and preparing our future. This is a book about how a society grows. This is a story about humankind and our advancement both individually and collectively.

Recently I attended a state council meeting. A trust had provided $5 million to answer the questions about improving the quality and accessibility of children's health care. These were good people with good intentions, but they were answering the same questions that were answered five years ago and fifteen. I watched as the words, "systems building, data analysis, outcome evaluation, project development, and technology management" rolled around in the presenter's mouth. As he clicked to the next Power Point presentation titled "Outcomes," I thought of my elementary school nurse, Mrs. Flood. It wasn't so long ago that she wore the pressed, white dress and the comfortable leather nursing shoes now replaced by neon-colored Crocs.

As the topic moved to increasing children's immunizations through an expanded database, I was wondering how a list of names or a column of numbers would ensure that children got the medical services they needed? In my school it was Mrs. Flood who made the calls home to parents. In fact, my school nurse met six of the eight objectives on this council's list, including oral and medical health care, increased number of children with health care coverage, home/coordinated approach, and fewer uninsured children. Through health care education and preventative examinations for head lice, scoliosis, and cavities, it was the school nurse who attended to our health. She also diagnosed my mononucleosis, called me at home three times during chicken pox, and saw that I got to the hospital after a broken finger. School nurses are a thing of the past. Recent legislative testimony revealed that the ratio of school district nurses is one nurse to two thousand students. It's the school secretaries who now tend to our children's injuries and infections, administer medications, and watch for physical abuse, sexual abuse, and neglect.

As the last Power Point slide comes into focus, I try and imagine five years from now. Will we still be spending our money on Power Points, conversations, and advisory councils, even though school nurses are cheaper and more effective? Will we be engrossed with controlling the outcomes, or improving them? Will we be tracking the children, or treating them? Now let's turn to the subject of education and bring a spoon.

❧ 1 ❧

High-Stakes Testing— What's Really at Stake

I'm no different than the majority of Americans who hate standardized tests. Countless books have been written criticizing the obvious—that bubbles do not represent intellect, and numeric scores do not begin to capture a person's range of knowledge or skills.

Tests such as the ACT, SAT, and most recently the GRE have never reflected my true abilities. Of course, there was that one test where I scored "100" and quite possibly changed the course of my life . . .

After middle school, I attended North High School, the public school in my area. There were more than five hundred students in my freshman class. That school still has the highest dropout rate in all of Denver, graduating only one-third of the initial ninth graders. As a white student, I was in the minority group. North High School offered accelerated classes, but my advisor placed me in Freshman English. Apparently the essay I'd written didn't earn me a seat in the advanced class (sentence diagramming in my Catholic middle school did not pay off).

It was in my freshman English class that I received a one hundred—my highest score ever on any classroom test. The test was a fill-in-the-blank exam. In some cases we were asked to look at the sentence and tell what part was incorrect based on the four possible options provided. I barely remember even looking at the questions.

After the teacher scored the tests, she pulled me and another student aside. She wanted to tell us that we had scored so well on the exam she was recommending that we be moved to Advanced English. She suggested that we think about if we wanted to move, since it was already three weeks into the school year. I asked what was different about the advanced class, and she

5

replied that it was mostly reading books and writing essays. I couldn't wait; all we'd been reading for those past three weeks was disconnected sentences out of uninteresting workbooks. I was sick and tired of fill-in-the-blank questions and short excerpts. I wanted to read real stories about meaningful things with actual characters and involved plots. We were instructed to think about it, but I was ready to sign on right then.

John, the other "perfect" score, was more reluctant. He didn't think we would do well in the advanced class because the reason we both got such high scores was because the teacher had accidentally passed out the answer sheet with John's test. The two of us had copied down the right answers. Yes, we cheated. Even so, I saw my opportunity. John elected to stay in the regular class, but I moved into the advanced class and so began my writing career. I was still only a C student, but I wasn't bored anymore—and I believe it was then, among all of those novels and essays, that I came to understand the power of words.

I think back to what might have happened had I not been provided the answer sheet. I would have forever been confined to the mediocre track, weighted down with practice books and remedial exercises. As it was, I stayed in the accelerated classes, even when I transferred schools. It was in those classes that I felt smart, because I was treated like I was smart, and soon I believed it too. The teachers in the advanced classes trusted us to think and be creative, and they challenged us to extend ourselves beyond what the "regular students" were being asked to do.

John, like so many of my peers, never graduated from high school. Too often our educational system involves barriers to achievement rather than real opportunities to think and learn.

A Different Shade of Gray

Most of us experienced standardized testing at one time or another during our education. We remember sharpening #2 pencils and shading in computer-generated circles on the answer sheets. Part of the reason today's testing has gone unquestioned is that standardized tests were such a benign aspect of our own schooling.

Today's "high-stakes" testing is much different than the kind of test-taking experiences of previous generations. For children growing up today with statewide performance standards and testing, the stakes are much higher. The No Child Left Behind (NCLB) act, the practice of grading schools based on students' test scores, performance pay, grade retention, and graduation exit exams have all made today's standardized testing a much different game.

A Step Back in History

Standardized testing got its roots in France in 1904. Under the commission of the French government, psychologist Alfred Binet and his young colleague, Theophile Simon, set out to identify children who had mental disabilities or were unable to learn in a traditional classroom setting.[1] Parisian schools were overcrowded because of newly instituted compulsory education laws, and schools were being forced to open their doors to poor, foreign, and children with disabilities for the first time. The schools in France were not equipped to deal with this new influx of children, many of whom came from uneducated families and generations of illiteracy.

Binet and Simon's efforts to differentiate children led to a revolutionary approach to evaluating individual mental ability and the development of the Simon-Binet Scale. According to Binet, the purpose of the scale was to assist children who required special education and not to rank or condemn a child to a permanent "condition."[2] He discounted the notion that intellect could be expressed as a fixed number because, he said, "intellect cannot be measured as linear surfaces are measured."

A German psychologist, William Stern, adopted exactly such a "fixed number" approach when he conceived of the intelligence quotient (IQ). Binet warned that to translate intellect as a single score or predictor would negatively affect children, their education, and their livelihood: "Some recent thinkers . . . [have affirmed] that an individual's intelligence is a fixed quantity, a quantity that cannot be increased. We must protest and react against this brutal pessimism; we must try to demonstrate that it is founded on nothing."[3]

Eugenics in America, 1910–1930:
Heredity as an Indicator of Nothing

Unfortunately, America's most influential educational researchers and policymakers of the time did not heed Binet's warnings. At the beginning of the twentieth century, the eugenics movement captured the interests of many Americans, resulting in one of the most damaging experiments in the history of public education. As the United States underwent rapid social and economic change, and as the nation became more industrial and urban, millions of immigrants from southern and Eastern Europe fled to the shores of America in hopes of opportunity and a better life. At the same time, thousands of African Americans were beginning a great migration to northern cities. As competition over jobs intensified, so did the friction along class and racial lines. Eugenics fed off the fears of white middle- and upper-class Americans and legitimized racial intolerance on a fabricated claim of science.

Eugenicists in Germany and elsewhere applied a flawed and crude interpretation of Gregor Mendel's laws on heredity. Mendel, an Austrian Augustinian monk, originally published his findings, "Experiments with Plant Hybrids," in 1864. In experiments with crossing garden peas, he developed a theory on organic inheritance.[4] American and German eugenicists misused Mendel's theory to argue that criminality, intelligence, and pauperism were passed down in families as simple dominant or recessive hereditary traits.[5] Charles Davenport, founder of the Eugenics Foundation, argued in favor of laws that would regulate the "spread of inferior blood" into the general population. In addition to the passage of the Immigration and Restriction Act of 1924, which established racist quotas, thirty states passed involuntary sterilization laws that targeted the blind, deaf, epileptic, "feebleminded," and paupers.

Public education was integral to the eugenics movement, and schools became the place where teachers and then children were indoctrinated into eugenic principles. Lewis Terman, a cognitive psychologist and eugenicist, invented the Stanford-Binet Intelligence Test as the means for tracking children into the "appropriate" job track. In his calculations, Terman adopted William Stern's version of the intelligence quotient. Most modern IQ tests calculate the intelligence quotient differently. The following excerpt is from Terman's teachers' training manual, *The Measurement of Intelligence* (1916):

> Among laboring men and servant girls there are thousands like them [feebleminded individuals]. They are the world's "hewers of wood and drawers of water." And yet, as far as intelligence is concerned, the tests have told the truth. . . . No amount of school instruction will ever make them intelligent voters or capable voters in the true sense of the word. . . . The fact that one meets this type with such frequency among Indians, Mexicans, and negroes suggests quite forcibly that the whole question of racial differences in mental traits will have to be taken anew and by experimental methods.
>
> Children of this group should be segregated in special classes and be given instruction which is concrete and practical. They cannot master, but they can often be made efficient workers, able to look out for themselves. There is no possibility at present of convincing society that they should not be allowed to reproduce, although from eugenic point of view they constitute a grave problem because of their unusually prolific breeding.[6]

Many researchers, scientists, and educators criticized eugenicists for misusing scientific principles to promote a racist agenda. Horace Mann, for example, spoke out against practices that legitimized discrimination and segregation and caused further harm to minorities and children born into poverty:

> But so long as any group of men attempts to use these tests as funds of information for the approximation of crude and inaccurate generalizations, so long we must continue to cry "Hold!" To compare the crowded millions of New York's East Side with the children of Morningside Heights [an upper-class neighborhood at the time] indeed involves a great contradiction; and to claim that the results of the tests given to such diverse groups, drawn from such varying strata of the social complex, are in any ways accurate, is to expose a fatuous sense of unfairness and lack of appreciation of the great environmental factors of modern urban life.[7]

Despite the protests of the use of manmade tests to rank and alienate racial and social groups, eugenics moved forward. By the early 1920s more than 2 million American schoolchildren were being tested for academic tracking purposes.[8]

The Rebirth of Standardized Testing

By the 1960s, much of the bias in the construction of standardized tests had become widely publicized, and testing children as a viable means of selection had been disproved. The civil rights movement banished many of the racial barriers and led to greater opportunities for minorities.

Although standardized tests were no longer being used to track students, some schools (likely out of habit) continued sporadic use of standardized tests such as the Iowa Test of Basic Skills (ITBS). Various districts administered normative standardized tests in two or three grade levels, but the data were considered an inadequate determinant of teaching or learning. Individual and schoolwide decisions were based on a multitude of variables and assessments and not solely on the basis of test scores, as they are now.

As standards-based education came into fashion, standardized test scores became the "ultimate" in desired outcomes. The 2002 federal education mandate, No Child Left Behind, returned children to the high-stakes game of standardized testing reminiscent of the eugenics era. According to the rules of NCLB, test scores are collected according to a child's race; each category of race must then show a 1 percent increase (or higher, depending on the state) each year, or the entire school is failed. NCLB mandates that all students in grades three through eight be "proficient" in reading and arithmetic according to the statewide test by 2014. Schools are penalized, teachers are sanctioned, and in the case of exit exams and retention policies, children are denied opportunities and advancement on the sole basis of a test score.

Tests as "scientific absolutes" have regained the popularity once attained in the 1920s. This time they are trusted to do more than quantify the intellect of children; now they are trusted to indicate the quality of a school and the effectiveness of the teachers. Testing every child is once again at the thrust of yet another American education reform movement.

I was part of the first group of educators to administer the Colorado Student Assessment Program (CSAP). My fourth grade students were exceptional writers, thoughtful, creative, organized, and descriptive with their essays. Reading and writing were a priority in my classroom, and as their teacher, I dedicated a great deal of time for both. The first time I administered the state standardized test in 1996, I didn't have any concerns about how my students would perform.

During the exam, Jeffrey (one of my most exceptional learners) walked over to where I was sitting, his faced flushed crimson. "Mrs. Engel, they want me to write an essay about some stupid alien."

"I know, Jeff; you are so creative, I'm confident that you can come up with a great story," I replied sympathetically.

"It's just that I was hoping for something more." The truth was, so was I. As adults, these students would be faced with major challenges, including global warming, overpopulation, disease, war, and a multitude of economic, social, and political challenges. I had worked all year to develop their skills and expand their knowledge so they would be prepared to solve the real-world problems they would someday have to face. Yet, here was the primary indicator of their ability and my teaching, asking them to write an essay about a friendly alien. My response to Jeff was, "I understand, but this topic may give you the opportunity to stretch your imagination."

His shoulders sunk, the red in his cheeks grew pale, and he muttered "I guess" and returned to his seat. I watched him sit and stare at the wall as the clock ticked on. With only ten minutes of the test remaining, he finally began to write. When I got the scores for the test (which was the next year), Jeffrey—my most gifted writer—had received the writing score of "unsatisfactory." In 2000, when the Colorado legislature voted to mandate CSAP for all students in grades three to ten and label schools based on CSAP test scores, I wrote to every single legislator.

Standardized Testing in Brief

Standardized simply implies that stimuli, instructions, scoring of test items, and proctoring procedures will be identical, with students taking the same test under the same conditions.[9] In general, there are two types of standardized tests: achievement tests, and cognitive abilities tests. *Achievement tests* measure students' responses compared with a predetermined set of subject matter and skill requirements for a particular grade level. *Cognitive abilities tests* (also known as *aptitude tests*) attempt to measure students' thought processes, such as verbal ability and reasoning skills. The majority of today's state standardized tests fall into the category of achievement tests.

Norm-Referenced Tests

Standardized tests also differ in the way that they are scored and reported. *Norm-referenced tests* (NRTs) measure students' answers in comparison with other students' answers from a "normal" group, ordinarily at the same grade level or in the same age group.

An NRT is scored so that 50 percent of students score above the midpoint (or average) and 50 percent score below. The test is specifically designed so that not every student can be successful in order to selectively order or rank children along a bell curve. Politicians who call for all students to score above the national average fail to understand NRT's guarantee that half of the test takers will fall below average. The expectation that all children score above the national average is like asking all Olympic runners to get a medal in their race. Although NRTs are still riddled with bias, the questions are all multiple choice, and scoring is done by a computer, making the evaluation process more objective (although not necessarily more accurate). With NRTs, it is important to know the composition of the norming group. The size of the group is much less important than the degree to which it is representative of the population being measured. Standardized tests that are NRTs include the Metropolitan Achievement Test (MAT); the Tests of Academic Proficiency (TAP); the Iowa Test of Basic Skills (ITBS); the California Achievement Test (CAT); the Comprehensive Test of Basic Skills (CTBS), which includes the "Terra Nova"; and the Stanford Achievement Test. IQ tests, "school readiness" and "cognitive ability" tests, and developmental screenings are also NRTs.

Criterion-Referenced Tests

Criterion-referenced tests (CRTs) measure student answers against a predetermined set of criteria and a preconceived notion of achievement rather than against other students. Criterion-referenced standardized tests are primarily multiple-choice but also include a few short-answer questions. Writing portions of the test may include an essay response.

The majority of state tests are standards based, meaning that test developers attempt to align test items with state standards. Test validity is determined according to whether the questions match the standards, not on the quality of questions or the accuracy of grading. Standards are often broad and ambiguous, leaving room for a variety of interpretations. Statewide tests provide only vague and generalized feedback, most often in the form of labels such as "above-proficient," "proficient," "partially proficient," or "unsatisfactory."

The Kentucky Instructional Results Information System (KIRIS), Colorado Student Assessment Program (CSAP), Georgia High School Graduation Test (GHSGT), Delaware Student Testing Program (DSTP), and Washington Assessment of Student Learning (WASL) are all examples of criterion-referenced tests.

The Question of Importance

The following sample of a criterion-referenced test demonstrates the irrelevance of the questions and the subjectivity of the answers on state standardized tests.[10]

"Egrets," by Judith Wright

As I traveled through a quiet evening,
I saw a pool, jet-black and mirror still.
Beyond, the slender paperbarks stood crowding;
Each on its own white image looked its fill,
and nothing moved but thirty egrets wading—
thirty egrets in a quiet evening.

Once in a lifetime, lovely past believing,
your lucky eyes may light on such a pool.
As though for many years I had been waiting,
I watched in silence, till my heart was full
of clear dark water, and white trees unmoving,
and whiter yet, those egrets wading.

21. The phrase "mirror still" emphasizes that the pool is
(a) dark and flowing.
(b) flat and calm.
(c) clean and transparent.
(d) round and full.

22. What does the phrase "lovely past believing" mean in the poem?
(a) impressive
(b) gigantic
(c) curious
(d) lucky

23. The speaker of the poem states, "I watched in silence, till my heart was full of clear dark water." Write an explanation to tell what the speaker means.

24. There are two stanzas in this poem. Why is this division appropriate for the poem?

Student responses to questions 23 and 24 are short-answer questions to be scored by seasonal testing employees who render their judgments based on a panel's stated criteria. Scoring personnel score literally hundreds of varied student responses each day under severe time constraints. In George Hillocks's book *The Testing Trap*, he describes the process for scoring the Illinois test. A company in North Carolina, which supervised the process, trained its temporary evaluators to grade each writing test essay on a thirty-two-point scale within sixty seconds.[11] Many scoring personnel lack university degrees or education experience, and the high volume of tests allows very little time to conduct careful evaluations.

This type of questioning also interferes with a child's active, creative, and rational learning process. The entire point of literature is that it is interpretive. There are no "right answers" in responding to poetry. This exercise of reading poetry and selecting the right answer is the kind of misguided and misinformed exercise that negates children's multidimensional thinking and fails to engender a sense of personal responsibility for their own learning.

When it comes to expectations from teachers and parents, we are looking for competence. For example, shaded bubbles can't tell us that a pilot can successfully land a plane each time. As Dr. William Spady explains, one-dimensional thinking is to "know something." Three-dimensional thinking is to know something and be able to apply it in context under conditions that reflect real life.[12]

Scientifically Objective—Please!

There is nothing empirical about a standardized test. It is written, evaluated, and graded by human beings, who are just as capable of error as the subjects they are testing. Because student evaluation and educational judgment have been diverted away from professional teachers and placed in the hands of test publishers, shouldn't we then be asking how they are being held accountable?

Martin Swaden of Edina, Minnesota, asked to see the test his daughter had failed—a test that prevented her from graduating in 2000. He had to threaten to sue before he was able to sit down with a state official, the test, and his daughter's answer sheet. Mr. Swaden found six errors that were incorrectly scored by National Computer Systems (now named NCS Pearson), the third-largest testing company in the country. The state determined that errors by NCS had caused 47,000 Minnesota students to get lower scores than they deserved, 8,000 to fail when they should have passed, and 525 seniors to be unjustly denied diplomas.[13] In retrospect, it has likely been errors such as the Minnesota test failure that ultimately caused the testing industry to operate under such a veil of secrecy.

National Computer Systems also incorrectly lowered multiple-choice scores for 12,000 Arizona students. In another incident, NCS was a forced to rescore 204,000 tests in Washington because the state found the scores too generous.

In recent years, the four major testing companies have experienced serious breakdowns in quality control.[14] One error by McGraw-Hill resulted in nearly 9,000 students in New York City being mistakenly assigned to summer school in 1999.[15] In 2002 in Nevada, 736 sophomores and juniors were mistakenly notified that they'd failed the state's proficiency exam that must be passed to earn a high school diploma.[16]

Florida retains thousands of children each year on the basis of their test scores. Yet in 2006, all third-grade FCAT reading tests had to be rescored. The concern was that the scores were "unfairly inflated," leading to the promotion of nine-year-olds "who should have otherwise been held back."[17] "Testing specialists argue that educators and politicians must share the blame for the rash of testing errors because they are asking too much of the industry," writes Henriques Steinberg.[18] I agree. However, in terms of accountability, we are also not asking nearly enough.

On March 12, 2006, headlines from the Associated Press read "More Colleges Rethinking SAT" after 4,000 SAT exams taken in October had been inaccurately scored.[19] Universities and colleges around the country are deemphasizing standardized test scores at a time when K–12 education is being dominated by them. According to FairTest, 740 accredited bachelor-degree granting colleges do not use the SAT (or ACT) to make admissions decisions about a substantial number of their applicants.[20]

Though we have instituted performance standards for children, we have not established standards and regulations for developing and scoring state standardized tests. Testing contractors and state policymakers apply their own methodology and create their own procedures for calculating and quantifying test results, which vary from state to state at an enormous expense and with a great deal of inaccuracy.

High Costs, Little Benefit

Efficiency appears to be a key word in the debate over educational reform and high-stakes testing. The idea that children could be "efficiently processed" through our educational system like Wal-Mart goods across price scanners is idiotic. Still, the total quality management drum beats on at the expense of taxpayers and our very own children.

There is nothing economical about evaluating schools with standardized tests. Contracts for state tests range in the millions. Testing contracts only include the fees for the development, publishing, and scoring of the test. The expensive burden of teacher training, test-prep materials, and time spent preparing students to score well on the test, proctoring these lengthy tests, processing the testing forms, organizing the data, and distributing the results, is shouldered by the school district—that is, taxpayers.

The General Accounting Office predicts that states will spend between $1.9 and $5.3 billion per year meeting the testing requirement of NCLB—a conservative estimate by all accounts. Testing is only a fraction of the cost of complying with the NCLB mandate; other provisions are even more expensive and, to the suddenly burgeoning education industry, even more lucrative."[21] According to Section 1116 of NCLB, schools identified for improvement must dedicate 10 percent of their Title I money to "scientifically based research," "specific annual measurable objectives," and "professional development." Corporations customize their educational product lines in response to government mandates, or, as we've seen in recent scandals, it's the other way around.[22]

In today's world, time is money. If you are disturbed by the amount of money being absorbed by the standardized testing industry, you may very well be outraged by the amount of time administrators, teachers, and students are spending on these single measures. Test sessions vary but average about fifty minutes, and students undergo between six and twelve test sessions. It's common for classes to spend one to three weeks taking state standardized tests, not including preparation time. Eight-year-olds are spending more time taking state tests than adults are required to spend on either the Law School Admission Test (LSAT), Graduate Record Exam (GRE), or the bar exam.

High-stakes testing may have come from the efficiency movement, but looking at the costs spent on standardized tests and the time invested preparing the test takers, there's clearly nothing "efficient" about it.

How High Are the Stakes?

Twenty-four states have made passing standardized tests a requirement for graduation.[23] Standardized tests are now being wielded like a weapon, creating barriers to long-term opportunity and real-life achievement. A study of the Texas accountability system, where NCLB originated, determined schools would group children into three categories: safe cases, suitable cases for treatment, and hopeless cases. Students in the safe cases were expected to pass the test. Students in the hopeless cases were not expected to pass the test or increase aggregate pass rates (remember the 1 percent mandated increase). In the Texas study, resources were directed away from both groups of "safe" and "hopeless" and toward suitable cases, "bubble kids" that were deemed helpful in raising school scores.[24]

Alice Miller, child psychologist, writes that "deciding what is good for a child and then forcing this so-called good on them by any coercive means possible is highly damaging to personal integrity and rational thought."[25]

Teachers in Greeley, Colorado, were handed a manual for administering the statewide test, the Colorado Student Assessment Program. The following is an excerpt taken from the manual *What We Really Need to Know About CSAP*:

> If a student appears to be ready to throw up before the test begins, call me and the child may come to the Health office and may take the test at another time. If the child needs to throw up in the middle of the test, pull a trash can by his/her side, let them "do their thing," and encourage the child to finish the test. If we allow the child to leave the room, they may not finish the test at a later date.

In the Aberdeen School District in Washington State, a fourth grader was suspended from school for five days following what the principal described as "blatant defiance and insubordination." The student completed the WASL test but was confused and did not answer one of the essay questions on the written portion of the WASL. According to the child, he found the wording confusing and didn't understand the question. The rules of administering the test are that teachers cannot provide any clarification or interpretation. The student did not complete the essay question and was suspended from May 9 to 13, 2005. In a letter to the child's mother, the principal of Central Park School states that the consequence of the student's "decision" not to answer the WASL task is a "particularly egregious wound" to other students and the school.

Most tragic is the climate that is cultivated under the conditions of high-stakes testing. Fear and oppression are a distinct contrast to the empowered citizenry imagined by public education's founding engineers.

One mother writes of her experience with her five-year-old son and the Dynamic Indicators of Basic Early Literacy Skills

(DIBELS) standardized test used in their Vermont kindergarten class:

> My son entered Kindergarten in my local public school in 2002. The school had just been refurbished and the old K classes were redesigned to make the room into an academic class. Part of the new K program included no recess or playing. I was not informed of these changes. I thought the empty shelves would be filled with various activities and games to improve the students' emerging skills.
>
> When he entered school it was my belief his reading skills were progressing naturally. He enjoyed being read to from various sources. Reading was a treasured part of our home life. He owned his own Pooh Bear diary. He was using scribbles to represent words/sentences and had filled out most of his diary. He knew the letters in his name yet still needed to improve his fine motor skills to print the letters more clearly. I thought everything was moving along just fine.
>
> His behavior changed over the school year. First, he did not want to go to school anymore. Next, he wanted to be rid of his beloved Pooh Bear diary. His reason was that only babies scribble. (His teacher had told the class this in desperation to get them to print regardless of their fine motor skills.) After this he did not attempt printing or scribbling anymore. Then he became obsessed with stopwatches and desperately wanted me to buy him one. Lastly, the true dagger hit my heart, he no longer wanted to read books with me.
>
> Towards the end of the school year I received a letter stating that he was going to require an intensive and expensive summer school program due to his low reading scores on something called a DIBELS test. As a former public school teacher, I was confused because I never had heard of this test. The letter contained very little information regarding his scores or the test. I began to wonder: What did the scores represent? What type of test was this? Why was I not informed that they were using this test?
>
> I researched the test on-line to learn more. The sites I did find appeared to be so similar to the state tests that my special education students at the high school level had been taking. The same type of lingo was used to promote how excellent this test was and how our children would become the best.

The site also explained how this test was going to be a nation-wide test. I was faced with more shiny propaganda. I already knew the damage the high school testing had done to educational environment and my students!

I also discovered that I could not find scientific testing or research concerning whether the test actually tested what it claimed to test. I found out that the children were timed, hence the burning desire for my son to own a stopwatch. He was never one for doing things in a speedy manner. I found out that my district was pulling him out [of] classes almost daily and doing practice timed testing using those ridiculous test items. I could just picture my sweet little boy sitting at a table and being timed to do X, Y and Z. I could see him looking at the stopwatch wondering how it worked and what it would feel like to push the buttons. He just loves gadgets. Then "ding," time is up. You failed!

I disagreed with their approach to reading, which appeared to be based on this DIBELS test. The district claimed that their curriculum and DIBELS testing was phonics based yet it did not appear to be a true phonics based program to me. I was sent home long lists of sight words that he was suppose to memorize. I was supposed to log all the books I read to him which thanks to their program he no longer enjoyed. In addition, the letter and vowel sounds were introduced in a confusing, erratic manner. According to the test the most valued skills appeared to be the rapid identification of letters and rapid identification of sight words.

I had him tested by an independent educational tester to be told that it is too early to know if he has a reading problem, all for a $1,000.00![26]

These aren't isolated examples. Absurdities and cruelties related to high-stakes testing are popping up in headlines across the nation.[27] Thousands of children are being retained because of a flawed paradigm.[28] Critical decisions about schools and children are being made on the single basis of standardized test scores. In Texas, 40,182 students didn't receive their diplomas because of the TAKS test.[29] You can be confident that when the tests are flawed, the decisions made as a result of those tests will be flawed as well.

Other districts are using an incentive approach to high-stakes testing. Raffles for televisions and Game Boys are held to encourage students to do well on the test. Sporting event tickets, pizza parties, time off from school, scholarships, and various bribes are held out to students who comply with testing or deliver high test scores. The money that would be spent on field trips, text books, science lab materials, art supplies, musical instruments, libraries, computers, athletic equipment, and smaller class sizes is now being spent on standardized tests and incentives. Imagine the number of teachers that could be hired for the cost of all this number crunching.

An Alternative to Standardized Tests

There is an alternative to standardized tests. Authentic assessments have been challenged, debated, and tested. Emphasis on measuring learning and assessing students' understanding in an authentic context started to gain support in the 1980s and the early 1990s. Theodore Sizer and other educational authorities worked on the development of assessments that raised expectations and reflected real-world contexts.[30] He advocated for expanded opportunities for students to show, produce, defend, and demonstrate not only what they have learned but how they apply that understanding to address real-world problems. Standardized tests, however, have replaced Sizer's original idea of assessment and created a new definition of performance. The difference between standardized tests and assessments is significant.

The purpose of an authentic assessment is to provide teachers, students, and parents with direct, specific, and immediate feedback into a student's understanding and real-world abilities. Assessments are important for educators because they reflect on the effectiveness of their instruction. Personalized assessments help students monitor their own progress and direct their own process and outcomes. Authentic assessments also are important tools for keeping parents informed of their child's development through a variety of measuring tools and contexts. Parents learn a great deal more about their child's progress from reading student writing examples collected throughout the year than from a single test label.

Authentic assessments differ from standardized tests because they can be developed by professional teachers, the grade-level team, or even the district. Standardized tests are limited to paper and pencil, but authentic assessments vary in all ways imaginable—they may evaluate children verbally as well as through observations, demonstrations, surveys, problem solving, and performances. Assessments can range from a spelling test to an instrumental performance, and from observing children create geometric shapes out of toothpicks to a debate in which each student has to argue a position from a side of the Union or Confederate armies from the time of the Civil War.

Some authentic assessments are even standardized themselves, such as the Qualitative Reading Inventory (QRI).[31] This assessment is a "running record" that requires a student to choose a passage from two or three options and read aloud. The teacher then records any specific errors and asks a series of comprehension questions at the end. Following along as the child reads, the teacher records self-corrections, phonics strategies, word substitutions, and additional diagnostic information that assist both the student and the teacher and informs instructional modifications.

When I administered the QRI to my fourth graders, I audiotaped the assessment at the beginning of the year and then again at the end. Students would listen to the tapes and look over their errors recorded on the written reading passages. They would then provide a summary of their own progress as well as a plan for improvement. Although QRIs are standardized, evaluations are specific to the individual student and extend beyond a simple label. All of the reading passages are leveled so that grade-level progress can be tracked over time. These kinds of assessments are much more effective than state standardized tests. They provide diagnostic information rather than merely indicating passing or failing. Results are also immediately available, instead of the following year when the class has moved on, as is the custom with state tests. Authentic assessments are administered in the classroom context under safe conditions, evaluated by trained and experienced educators, and provide comprehensive feedback to students, teachers, parents, and administrators.

In contrast, standardized tests provide only a raw score or brand that provides little evidence or insight into children's abilities and their developmental process. Today's state standardized tests and authentic assessments can be distinguished by a single indicator: purpose. If the purpose of the assessment, in terms of development and application, is to assess students' knowledge and application of that knowledge, it is worthwhile. If the purpose is to label students, schools, and teachers, it is simply a government exercise with no value.

It's Broken—Fix It!

Proponents and supporters of high-stakes testing promised that standards and tests would improve schools and raise student achievement. It hasn't happened. In the seven years since NCLB was enacted, thousands of schools have been reconstituted or closed, the curriculum has narrowed, and drop-out rates have increased. Colleges and universities are also complaining that this new generation of test-takers arrives at college ill equipped and in need of remediation. Test preparation has become a replacement for today's curriculum rather than a simple measure of it. A survey by the Center on Education Policy found that since the passage of NCLB, 71 percent of the nation's 15,000 school districts had reduced the hours of instructional time spent on history, music, and other subjects to allow more time for reading and math, the two subjects of statewide tests.[32] The manufacturing model has spread from our industrial plants to our classrooms, where it is not working.

If it's not broken, don't fix it; but if it is broken—and it most certainly is—fix it! Not only is high-stakes testing the wrong answer, but the continual obsession with test scores in the United States keeps us from seeking the right answers for quality schools and the children they are designed to serve.

Great public schools are the best hope for our future. When we, as a nation, allow conformity over individualism, profit at the expense of progress, and measurement above meaning, we have diminished our capacity for greatness and limited our own potential for the extraordinary.

From Standards to Standardization

When standards-based instruction first came to my school district, I was thrilled. It was my goal to be the first teacher in the school to implement standards-based instruction. Within a couple of years I had realigned my entire curriculum to reflect the state and district standards. Parent conferences were redesigned around standards as well as student portfolios. It's interesting where the learning process can lead us.

Standards Defined

Standards is perhaps one of the most difficult concepts to define and has varying interpretations, even for people familiar with educational jargon. According to *Merriam-Webster's Collegiate Dictionary,* tenth edition, *standard* has twelve meanings, including this one: "sound and usable but not of top quality." A car that meets the standard wouldn't necessarily be considered the highest-rated vehicle.

The most commonly accepted definition of a standard as it relates to education is "something set up and established by authority as a rule for the measure of quantity, weight, extent, value, or quality."[1] In education, standards are a set of criteria established by a group of people. Sometimes the criterion is directed at what teachers will teach (content standards). In most cases today, the criterion defines what students will demonstrate (performance standards).

A Quick Walk Down Memory Lane

Willard Wirtz, former labor secretary during the Reagan administration, and Archie Lapointe made the following conclusions in their 1982 report entitled *Measuring the Quality of Education: A Report on Assessing Educational Progress*:

> By the early 1970's, the national sense developed that educational quality was deteriorating rapidly and dangerously. It is not entirely clear how far this went, how general it was, or what measure of fault was the schools. But the judgment was made clearly and firmly. The reaction to this alarm took a dramatically new form. For reasons rooted in other developments, many people had lost confidence in the government and in the professions. The strongly sensed deterioration in education seemed confirmation of the failures of both of these services. So it was decided not to rely this time on either of these agencies. The decision, instead, in one state and community after another, was to move in directly on the schools, not with funds, but with "standards."[2]

A Nation at Risk: A Report to the Nation,[3] released in 1983, described schools as failing and solidified the trend toward standardization. This eventually led to centralizing public schools under the authority of the federal government. Although the report relied on weak evidence, it contained strong rhetoric:

> If an unfriendly foreign power had attempted to impose on America the mediocre educational performance that exists today, we might well have viewed it as an act of war. . . . We have even squandered the gains in student achievement made in the wake of the Sputnik challenge. Moreover, we have dismantled essential support systems which helped make those gains possible. We have, in effect, been committing an act of unthinking, unilateral educational disarmament.[4]

Though never supported by research,[5] the report was met with general acceptance by the broad public. By the mid-1980s, after *A Nation at Risk* had been widely promoted in the media, the public was carrying the chant of "failing schools." Proponents of standardization were able to advance their position on the claim that the lack of regulation in the educational system was to blame for deteriorating schools. The solution they proposed was to regulate student learning through standards and ultimately to monitor teachers through standardized tests.

Bill Clinton's *Goals 2000* began the first national mandate toward standardization.[6] In the mid-1990s numerous governors began to call for state standards. By the turn of the century, all fifty states had implemented a uniform, homogenized, standardized curriculum.

Same Ol' Same Old

Before standardization reforms, states already had grade-level or subject curriculums in place. Some curriculums were statewide whereas other states honored local governance, in which case the curriculum guidelines, developed by educators and elected school board members, were unique to each individual district.

Content standards aren't really a new concept. Established criteria for what basic concepts should be taught in classrooms have always been predetermined. In fact, curriculums and grade-level guidelines have been in place since the inception of the one-room schoolhouse. When a professional accepted the position of teacher, he or she would be provided a curriculum guide listing concepts to be taught, a grade book in which to record assessments of students' acquisition of the material, and perhaps a switch or paddle to ensure compliance. Reading, writing, and arithmetic, the core skill set, were consistently taught in every schoolroom from countryside to countryside.

Population growth and expansion brought new communities and new school districts. Some districts developed more quickly than others, and as time progressed, the curriculum guides grew more detailed and comprehensive. For example, an Alabama curriculum guide from 1964, prior to "standards-based reforms," is 482 pages long for grades 7 to 12. English, social studies, health and physical education, mathematics, science, foreign languages, business education, fine arts, counseling services, the library, and educational television are all addressed in the *Alabama Course of Study*.[7] According to the introductory letter, "Over one thousand Alabama educators participated either in developing or in appraising and reviewing"[8] the state curriculum over a four-year period. This *Course of Study* exemplifies the value of professional involvement and feedback from teachers in planning and coordinating classroom instruction and expectations, prior to the doctrines of standards-based government mandates.

Of all of the research I've uncovered, this curriculum guide developed for every high school in the state of Alabama is the most compelling example of how students have been held accountable to well-defined expectations long before standardization reforms. Yes, content standards have been done before, and they've been done better.

Learning from Experience

What I learned in my own classroom is that although there is nothing new about standards, "standards-based education reform" creates completely different learning opportunities and environments for children.

My experience with implementing performance standards illustrated the unintended consequence associated with attempts to standardize human beings. The year before I adopted the state's definitions of standards, I had designed my entire fourth-grade curriculum with a focus on Colorado history (the district social studies curriculum requirement). The culminating event was a two-day camping trip to South Park, Colorado. We visited a mine, a railroad roundhouse, and a walking museum depicting early Colorado. Parents and speakers were brought in throughout the year to make presentations and help with instruction. Reading, writing, math, science, geography, history, and even the study of government and civics were all integrated in our studies.

In language arts, the children read nonfiction books and learned how to research and integrate sources. One project involved choosing a famous Colorado person and writing a five-paragraph essay using three sources. Students learned how to access and organize their research, identify important and supporting details, and synthesize the information in their own words. The public was invited as the children, dressed in costume, acted out the role of their famous person in our "living wax museum."[9]

In math, students determined a budget for our trip, calculated mileage, studied maps, determined the shortest route, planned the schedule, identified expenses, allocated supplies, and solved problems around population, altitude, and so forth.

In science, we studied ecosystems, plant and animal biology, rocks and minerals, waterways, simple machines related to the development of mining, and nutrition, including all meal planning and preparation.

We studied Native Americans and early settlers. The class even put on a mock trial in which the U.S. military was tried for the murders of sleeping Indians at the Sand Creek Massacre. Students learned about the three branches of government, and the head judge in our county visited our class to explain the trial process. The students cast their votes and elected the team of attorneys for the defense and prosecution, and every child was assigned a role. The trial included twelve witnesses, and the verdict was decided by a jury of peers (another class).

We explored the gold rush, trappers, the railroad, cities, attractions, floods, fires, and important events in Colorado's history. Students kept a resource book all year and compiled all sorts of fascinating information.

This type of instruction emphasized the process, though I considered the outcomes throughout my planning. My overall objective was for my students to develop an appreciation and historical understanding of their home state, Colorado. My instructional goal was to ensure that the learning experiences I facilitated improved the students' individual abilities to read, write, ask questions, solve problems, think critically, evaluate information, communicate, and work cooperatively. There were daily assessments to help children clarify and expand their understanding and to help me improve my instruction.

The final assessment was a photo journal—pictures taken by students during our expedition. Journal captions tied together all the research and information we had collected throughout the year. The students were required to share their photo journals with the class and explain what they personally had come to understand about Colorado and themselves throughout the process. In evaluating the journals, I used a rubric (established criteria for what constitutes each letter grade) that the class and I had developed together. For example, an A was given to photo journals that had detailed captions; integrated a variety of sources; contained accurate information; and were beautifully prepared, eloquently written, original, neat, organized, and turned in on time. Students were required to evaluate themselves before I completed my grading.

Children are surprisingly honest; I find they are more critical than generous in their self-reflections. What I also noticed through this particular assessment process was that although each child had developed an in-depth understanding of Colorado and the concepts presented, they each experienced and expressed their learning differently. Some children emphasized the history of Colorado whereas others focused on the natural resources or on influential people. Several students demonstrated their gift for writing with detailed and elaborate descriptions, and others exhibited visual images, rich photographs, drawings, timelines, and charts. They all were assigned the same project, but the results were as unique as the individuals. Some of my students' learning and understanding shone not in their journal but in their presentation.

Proponents of standardization are apt to consider this type of teaching to be a "pet project" or "fluff." I call it engaging, meaningful, and effective teaching. That entire year, my students couldn't wait to come to school, and I couldn't wait to greet them at the door! I remember one little girl crying because she had to be sent home with a fever. I pacified her with the promise of extra school work and sent her home to cartoons and chicken soup.

One Step Backward

Back in 1993, my teacher certification program at the University of Denver followed the trend of standards reform. At the time, standardization appealed to my sense of order, structure, and control. Once I was hired, my goal was to be the first teacher in my suburban school to implement an entirely standards-based classroom. I helped in the planning and development of my district's standards and checkpoints, carried the standardization flag, and called out the "accountability chant."

In my third year of teaching, I made the complete switch to a standardized classroom; subjects were compartmentalized along with the standards.[10] I redesigned all my lessons around the particular standards instead of a concept or theme as I had done with the Colorado unit. In science, for example, our district had nine standards and seventeen checkpoints. The standard and/or checkpoint would be written on the chalk board at the beginning of each of my lessons, and my "trainees" would recite the standard as the purpose for the lesson. For example:

Science standard #2C: The student demonstrates an understanding that interactions between matter and energy can produce changes in a system, although the total quantities of matter and energy remain unchanged.[11]

The difference between standards-based education and prior models is the unrelenting focus on immediate outcomes rather than the process. I would provide short exercises to accommodate the large number of benchmarks, in which my students would demonstrate the performance standard (outcome). Eventually I would have my students cut out the checkpoints or benchmarks and glue them to the top of their worksheets as evidence during parent–teacher conferences that they indeed had accomplished something. Which I later concluded was really nothing.

I've since come to discover that teaching children standards is like teaching adults tax codes. It's a government exercise with no real value to the individual. Each Spring American citizens learn enough to calculate the correct taxable amount in order to make their contribution and avoid an audit—that's all.

At the time of my standardization affliction, my district listed nearly forty standards and close to one hundred checkpoints just in the basic subjects. There are far more now, and the Colorado Department of Education has produced yet another volume of standards. The bureaucratic quagmire named "education standards" creates chaos and confusion for teachers and parents and translates to absolute nonsense for children.

Still, standardization scored me big points in the education profession. Eventually I was promoted to the position of academic director in an alternative Christian high school. One of my first projects was to align curriculum and assessments with state standards. I moved up the standardized ladder; my students moved down.

Again I watched firsthand the transition and effects of a standards-based education. Students are categorized, measured, labeled, and completely disassociated from their own learning. Parents are overwhelmed and frustrated. In the end, my experiences served to clarify how our attempts to quantify fail to address the qualities that matter most for our children and our society. Standardization and testing tools do not provide students the opportunity "to carry out extended analyses, to solve open-ended problems, or to display command of complex relationships, although these abilities are at the heart of higher-order competence," explains Lauren Resnick, a leading cognitive scientist.[12] Standardization offers a sanitary approach to education, but also a meaningless one.

Standards Applied

So here's where the arguments over standardization may get a little confusing. Standards, in and of themselves, are not the problem. Standards are only words on a page. The distinction is that while standards are not the problem, they are not the answer either. Reformers have grown distrustful of educators and the system of public education. Their answer has been to defer the responsibility of our children and their education to artificial mechanisms. Rather than empowering the people who implement the standards—school leaders, teachers, parents, and students—they direct all of the attention and resources toward the standards and the tools that measure those standards.

To further illustrate this distinction let's return again to the 1964 *Alabama Course of Study*,[13] grades 7–12. Under the heading "Grammar," read:

Grammar Objectives

- To teach skills needed to communicate intelligently, effectively, interestingly, and with ease. These skills are listening, thinking, speaking, reading, writing, spelling, and vocabulary building.
- To teach that which is fundamental and changeless and to teach that which is eclectic, which means making the best choice of words and expressions.
- To have an organized plan for the year's work, attempting to meet the needs of every student.
- To have sequence from year to year to reinforce retention of the basic facts taught.
- To organize instruction so that individuals, independently and in small groups, may learn to their full capacity.
- To vary the presentation of grammar each year to avoid unnecessary repetition.
- To teach with enthusiasm and command of the subject.
- To discriminate between the important and unimportant, emphasizing essential materials.

- To have a purpose in every assignment and a value in its accomplishment.
- To promote good English usage in all classes and not in English courses only.
- To encourage the use of good English outside the classroom.

According to the Alabama Department of Education, the following 2002 high school language arts performance standards, as measured by a statewide test, have now replaced the earlier grammar objectives:

STANDARD I: The student will recognize correct grammar and usage.

STANDARD II: The student will demonstrate appropriate word choice.

STANDARD III: The student will recognize correct sentence structure.

STANDARD IV: The student will use correct capitalization and punctuation.

STANDARD V: The student will use appropriate organizational skills for writing/revising.[14]

The transition from standards to standardization happened so gradually and so subtly that few recognize the change or the impact. The purpose of the 1964 standards was to improve education, guide and support teachers, and maximize students' learning. The purpose of today's student performance standards is to measure student outcomes. Why the importance of measuring, you ask? Because there is a belief, albeit flawed, that if you can measure the outcome, then you can control the outcome.

The micromanagement approach has standards driving state assessments, which drive school ratings, which drive instruction, curriculum, programming, scheduling, hiring, placement, and everything else. *Voilà!* There you have it; from standards to standardization. The sad truth is that greater control from federal and state governments has led to poor outcomes for both teachers and students.

Schools as well as businesses have learned that top-down management models hinder efficiency and hamper productivity. Charles Boettcher, one of the wealthiest and most successful businessmen of the Industrial Revolution, said, "There is nothing more important to business than the men who make it up. Machinery can be bought or repaired, or renewed, or rearranged, but the finest machinery in the world is worthless without good men to run it."[15] What was true during the Industrial Revolution is still true today. No machine, software package, policy, or procedure is greater than the people who operate and implement them.

If only we could remember that people are a nation's greatest asset. Accompanying Alabama's student performance standards now are prescribed lesson plans, developed according to the Alabama High School Graduation Exam (AHSGE), first implemented in 2001.[16] The example in the appendix is a lesson plan in which students in grade eleven are asked to sequence sentences from the story of *Goldilocks and the Three Bears*. These sixteen- and seventeen-year-olds aren't expected to write the sentences; instead, they are instructed to choose the "correct answers" from the numbered choices (see the full lesson in Appendix A). This example illustrates how we have reduced education to the lowest common denominator. Today's graduates will be faced with more career opportunities than any previous generation and not have an inkling of what to do with them.

Flawed Assumptions

The differences between earlier education standards and today's standardized education are most evident in the reforms underlying assumptions. Today's standards-based education reforms have developed out of the following assumptions:

- A universal body of knowledge exists that every child should acquire.
- The value of a school, a teacher, and a child is quantifiable.
- All children, despite their differences in personalities, abilities, interests, and experiences, will respond the same way to instruction.
- Learning is a product.
- A measurable education equals a quality education.
- Strict regulation of both educators and students will ensure compliance toward national and state goals.

None of these assumptions are accurate, and as a result, standards-based education is condemned by its own ideological framework. This next section closely examines the flawed assumptions and misguided intentions of today's standardized reforms.

Defining a Body of Knowledge— an Inappropriate Outcome

If you were to ask an engineer, a musician, a scientist, an investor, a preacher, an author, and a parent, "What body of knowledge should every child acquire?" the responses would be quite different. How is it, then, that each state has now decided what every child must know and demonstrate? In an attempt to define the "standards," states have been required to simplify, generalize, and place limitations around a body of knowledge to generate some degree of consensus.

The performance standards (uniform expectations) required for all children are, in fact, minimum competencies directed to a median population. E. D. Hirsh attempted to answer the question, "What should *every* child know and be able to do?" in his Core Knowledge curriculum.[17] The problem is that the very act of defining a body of knowledge for every student limits the academic experience and that child's intellectual capacity.

Human Beings Are Not Quantifiable

With the advancements of technology and the precision of science, we human beings have become far more sophisticated in our ability to measure things. Certainly science, measurement, and even outcome-based research have their place. Scientists testing materials for the space shuttle must study the outcomes of various temperatures, pressures, and chemical reactions. In those instances the conditions are controlled and the variables constant. In contrast, human beings differ, and so do their conditions. It is prudent to question, then, whether outcome-based research is ever truly reliable when the variables are so dissimilar and the generalized conclusions are applied to the masses. Many researchers would argue in the affirmative and, of course, would be out of business if the answer were different.

The reality is that we cannot accurately quantify every student using the same measurement tool. Standardization does not consider the countless variability associated with every individual human being. Take, for example, two random children born on the same day: if we feed them the exact same food and in the same quantity, they would not gain the same amount of weight. We know that level of activity, genetic traits, body chemistry, and metabolism are all variables that affect the body's ability to process nutrients.

The same applies for the mind's ability to process information. Parents and educators know the information and experiences of our children are far more difficult to quantify than the food they consume—because information and experience are not even raw materials. Not only is the federal application of standardized tests a misuse of assessments and the subsequent data; it is especially a misuse of our children and our teachers. Numbers-driven education reform is not evidenced-based research, and human beings are not quantifiable.

Children Are Different and Will Respond Differently

The goal of selecting performance standards and uniformly applying them to millions of children is entirely inappropriate because children are completely unique from one another—culturally, genetically, chemically, socially, emotionally, intellectually, and so forth. Psychometricians know that comparing children in early development stages is a vague science—profitable but vague.

Rather than improve education, reformers have undertaken the goal of aligning the standards with the tools that measure the standards. Some argue that the tests are measuring standards, and others argue that the tests are measuring students. I argue, "Who cares?"

Just because standardization works for toasters does not mean it works for human beings. Standards-based education resembles the factory assembly-line approach of regulating the inputs so as to maximize the outputs. Unfortunately, those who are intent on standardizing future generations fail to give credence to the essential differences between a factory and a classroom.

In a factory, the raw materials are identical. Put plastic and nylon into the machine, run the materials through a duplicative manufacturing process, and ta-da—out come toothbrushes! You may create some variation in colors, perhaps even design differences in shapes. The reality in a toothbrush factory is that when you control the input of raw materials and mechanize a repetitive assembly process, you control the product output.

Children are not toothbrushes, and children do not resemble anything close to identical "raw material." Boys and girls enter their classrooms preassembled—intellectually, emotionally, and physically. Standardization is a destructive means for relating to these boys and girls as well as an incompetent way of educating them.

Even if teaching could be absolutely standardized, or mechanized, we know that each child will listen, process, comprehend, and express that learning differently. There are so many variations in people that attempts to control and define us as mere products or outputs is not only impossible, it is absurd. Furthermore, the drive toward a universal mindset and skill set (standardization) is counter to a future that demands collaboration, ingenuity, and adaptability.

The oranges, bananas, mangos, and pineapples are all beginning to look more like apples. Standardized testing tools can measure apples against apples. At what cost to our children does this comparison come, and what are we going to do with so many apples?

Learning—Process or Product!

Minimum competencies are far more manageable than are we— you and me—living, breathing, complexly unique, and continuously developing. Learning, however, is very much a process. In the zeal to quantify and control, reformers have not only devoted themselves to getting the variables (children) to match up, but they have also attempted to convert their learning from a process into a product. Products, it is believed, will lend themselves to accurate measurements and control over an uncertain future.

With its intricate functions and vast capabilities, the brain is the most complex system in the human body. Although science has been unsuccessful at quantifying human potential, research has continued to reveal the immensity of the brain's capacity for processing information. Recognizing how and why we learn is essential to understanding how and why standards-based education undermines the learning process, narrows the range of thought, diminishes human potential, and, in the end, damages our schools and our children.

Human beings begin the learning process by gathering small bits of new information and attaching that knowledge to previously established frameworks. Over a period of time, new experiences and connections are formed, and understanding is developed. As Albert Einstein said, "The only source of knowledge is experience." It is from these varied experiences that new knowledge is reinforced and a more permanent understanding of the world around us is finally established.

Think back to when you first learned to ride a bike. It may have been a Big Wheel or tricycle when you learned how to pedal and to steer. As you grew, your experience and capacity improved, and you eventually moved to a two-wheeler with training wheels, cultivating a sense of balance. Continuing on, you grew in coordination, and the training wheels went away. Gradually, with practice and experience, you learned how to ride a bicycle. Finally, the saying, "Once you learn to ride a bike you never forget" becomes real, because the knowledge was developed incrementally over time, through personalized experience and with all biological systems engaged. Consider the process of learning how to ride a bicycle in contrast to shading bubbles on multiple-choice questions.

All learning, whether riding a bicycle or learning to read, is a process—one that is distinctly different for each individual. Just because a child does not remove his or her training wheels by the age of six does not mean he or she cannot ride a bike.

Standardization fails to consider that learning is a unique process, and so is the learner. Today's educational goals are no longer focused on developing adults who are readers, writers, problem solvers, investigators, citizens, neighbors, and so forth. Rather, the goal is now focused on manufacturing third graders who can:

- spell forty-two predetermined words correctly;
- write "proficiently" according only to test publishers and their temporary test graders; and

- read as measured by correct answers on thirty-two multiple choice and short-answer questions.

In the world of standardization, Children must disassociate from their own thinking process in order to produce the desired "product" to then be measured and then misconstrued, misinterpreted, and misreported.

A Measurable Education Does Not Equal a Quality Education

It is a great tragedy that American citizens associate high test scores with a quality school and conversely associate low test scores with failing schools. Rarely is there a newspaper editorial that can discuss the state of education outside of the context of numbers. Schools have replaced their librarians with data managers, and the spread sheets are plentiful. The cold reality is that those nifty little pie charts, bar graphs, and sound bites have not led us to better schools.

When I was a fourth grade student at Brown Elementary School in Denver, we participated in a study to determine how students learn typing skills. The widespread use of computers was growing, and educators were busy adjusting to the new technology. In this particular study, our school was given cardboard copies of a keyboard. Another school participating in the study was given actual keyboards, although not connected to anything. A third school was given functioning computers. I specifically remember my parents' frustration that my school (in a low-income area) received pictures of a keyboard and the school in the wealthiest neighborhood was given actual computers. Some things never change.

I can still recall those silly little exercises and my teacher saying, "Now move your left index finger on your card to the 'T' position." I never had the benefit of seeing the outcome of the study. I can only say that when I took typing in junior high, I had no advantage over those children who had been denied the privilege of the cardboard keyboard. Never again have I seen children learning computer skills on a piece of paper. I would be curious to find out how the students who practiced on keyboards, but weren't able to observe the results of their finger movements on a monitor, fared compared to those who worked on real computers.

When it comes to developing knowledge, children must be able to feel it, see it, talk about it, and let it roll around in their heads until this new piece of information attaches to something meaningful. Learning must be personal, worthwhile, and challenging if it is to engage the human mind. Standards are designed to be impersonal, uniform, and inflexible, thereby defying everything we know about the human brain and the innate desire for learning.

In his book *To Think*, Frank Smith explains,

> Thinking is easy and effective when two fundamental requirements are met. The first is the need to understand what we are thinking about; and the second is for the brain itself to be in charge, in control of its own affairs, going about its own business.[18]

Without a real-world connection and meaningful immediate feedback, the standardized exercise is comparable to learning bicycling on a stationary bike. Students are not engaged; their brains are not in control of their own affairs.

It is not a stretch to presume that children would not be motivated to learn on a bike that does not take them anywhere. In other words, if the final product is of no value to the student, then what's the point? Students can and have generated millions of correct answers on bubble sheets, but that won't solve an economic crises, keep a home from burning to the ground, or heal a dying a child. Numbers right or wrong, positive or negative, increasing or decreasing, will not guarantee a quality education.

Cultivating the varied talents and interests of students isn't nearly as neat as managing performance standards or as simplistic as administering a standardized test, but it is a basic requirement of developing the intellectual, physical, and social capacities of our youth.

Standardization—a Contradiction in American Values

The first mistake we have made in today's reforms is to emphasize the outcomes over the process. The second mistake has been to limit those outcomes by expecting identical responses from every child. The third and biggest mistake is that standards-based education has not informed the educational model but in fact replaced it.

As I write this chapter, discussion is under way in Washington, DC, to institute national standards and a new national standardized test. The suggestion of the government mandating uniform outcomes and a measurement tool that aggregates children according to race closely parallels Germany's national socialism and Italy's fascism.

Fascist states provide order, safety, and protection in an otherwise chaotic environment, and in return, all else is sacrificed to the state. Fascism calls for the complete subjugation of the individual. In his 1935 publication *Fascism Doctrine and Institutions*, Benito Mussolini described the relationship between citizen and state:

> The state, as conceived and realized by Fascism, is a spiritual and ethical entity for securing the political, juridical, and economic organization of the nation, an organization which in its origin and growth is a manifestation of the spirit. . . . Transcending the individual's brief spell of life, the State stands for the immanent conscience of the nation. The State educates the citizens to civism, makes them aware of their mission, urges them to unity; its justice harmonizes their divergent interests; it transmits to future generations the conquests of the mind in the fields of science, art, law, human solidarity; it leads men up from primitive tribal life to that highest manifestation of human power, imperial rule.
>
> But imperialism implies discipline, the coordination of efforts, a deep sense of duty and a spirit of self-sacrifice. This explains many aspects of the practical activity of the regime, and the direction taken by many of the forces of the State, as also the severity which has to be exercised towards those who would oppose this spontaneous and inevitable movement.[19]

National socialism during the 1930s bears a close resemblance to fascist principles. After the Nationalist Socialist Party seized power in 1933, its members quickly began reforming all aspects of the German education system. According to the Führer himself, "The future of the German nation depends on its youth. All German youth will therefore have to be prepared for its future duties."[20] Under the Third Reich, Germany saw the introduction of a national socialist curriculum that centralized German education. Teachers were subjected to intensive training on party standards and could be dismissed solely on the grounds that they might not "without reservation at all times act in the interest of the state."[21] Nazi officials reviewed textbooks for suitability and commissioned the publication of new materials heavily favoring eugenics. The following letter illustrates the implications of universal conformity and excessive state control.

Lina Haag, in her letter from the Lichtenburg concentration camp, describes the brutality of the German reeducation project:

> I have looked into terrible hearts and minds, into hearts that besides monstrous cruelty contained a disposition always inclined to sentimentality, and into minds that seemed harmless and simple and good-natured, but still were the minds of diligent executioners. We find it dreadful and disturbing that Hitler's creatures are not recruited from an asocial element, but from the lower middle-class element of the people. They are not born sadists, nor professional criminals, nor impassioned murderers, but just small-minded middle-class conformists.[22]

The danger of standardizing our public education system is not only that we mandated a "groupthink" mentality. Most concerning is that "the state" is determining the thinking of the group.

In a democracy, "It is not the function of our government to keep the citizen from falling into error; it is the function of the citizen to keep the government from falling into error," this according to the 1950 U.S. Supreme Court.[23] The idea of the federal government and its testing contracts controlling what our children will think, how they will learn, and what they will demonstrate counters the principles of liberty and democracy, ignoring the rich diversity and individualism that has distinguished America.

Differentiation Is the Answer

The history and the successes of the United States have been marked by ingenuity, invention, and imagination. Electricity, the automobile, the telephone, the radio, the airplane, modern computers, atomic energy, and wireless networks are all American inventions. The United States does not hold exclusive rights for development or discovery, but up until the past couple of decades we have been able to prevent the conditions that stifle such innovations.

Furthermore, the fact that we have attempted to apply a uniform, inflexible, and standardized approach to education shows either how little we know about children or how little we care. Yet, politicians, CEOs, school administrators, and—yes—even educators will go to great lengths to defend standardization. A great deal of money, time, and careers are invested in standardization's flawed paradigm.

Today every school, every classroom, every teacher, and every student is driven by a single test because it is the sole measure of success. Standards-based education is sold as the breakthrough cure in a rose-colored bottle, when it is hypochondria that creates the suffering. The reality of standardizing public school children is that human outcomes are impossible to mandate, accurate measurement tools don't exist, and even if we could and they did, it wouldn't matter anyway.

Still, it is going to take a lot for the decision makers to have to step out of auto-pilot and begin asking questions beyond how can we rewrite standards and how can we improve test scores. It is up to us now to ask them to go beyond measuring students and reporting data and begin improving schools and expanding learning opportunities for our children.

The answers are not out of reach. We know which children are getting short-changed and how. We've collected enough data over the decades to tell us small class sizes, involved parents, safe schools, highly competent and compensated teachers, quality resources, early intervention, and supportive communities make a difference in the lives of our children. Words on paper and questions on a test are not going to prepare our youth for their future. That is a responsibility that falls to us parents, teachers, and citizens.

The key to our nation's success is an educational system in which instruction is personalized, curriculum is challenging, and learning is both engaging and meaningful, not to every child but to each child. It is the opposite of standardization. A system that is process-oriented, student-driven, and varied enough to meet the needs of a highly diverse population—these are the standards that matter, even if they can't be measured. If we fail our educational system now, we will have done more than corrupt the minds and hearts of generations to come. We will have forfeited the viability of this entire nation.

What Really Counts

I remember when I was finally forced to face the reality of a standardized education. I was sitting amid my student portfolios, looking at all of the work my students had collected over the past eight months: writing samples, math problems, reading responses. It was fine work, but they hadn't chosen the examples that represented their best abilities or their proudest achievements as readers, writers, scientists, and mathematicians (civics wasn't even considered). Instead, they chose the work that matched the standard on the checklist I had given them. Their portfolios were extensive. They had taken hours to compile, organize, and present the prescribed outcomes.

So there I was, sitting on the floor and asking why—and finally asking, "What's it all for?" With the bitter taste of truth settling in, I came to terms with the knowledge that my students had done it all for me. When you boil it down, relationship is the most significant element of successful teaching and learning.

A year from now, my students wouldn't remember or care how the state or district had defined the standards. Why should they? There was no real value to those exercises—not for my students and, honestly, not for me either. Performance standards did not improve my teaching, and they most certainly did not improve my students' learning. Rather than having them all think alike and demonstrate that thinking in the same way, what I really desired was for my students to think for themselves and to apply the information and the experiences to their personal lives. Not in a way that the state could account for their performance, or my teaching, but in a way that their lives would account for what they had learned under my leadership.

❧ 3 ❧

Accountability Feigned

In 2000, the state of Colorado elected a new governor. His first order of business was to pass legislation that graded schools based on test scores and replace schools rated "low" with charter schools. At the time I was home, caring for my daughter Grace and her newborn sister, Sophie. The governor's act compelled me to write my first letter to a legislator, which concluded with these words:

> Let us be cautious in our approach to educational reform—we have much to lose. Before you cast your vote, I suggest you spend a week in a classroom that will be affected by the choices you make. You will also be held accountable for our children and the future of public education. Preparing our children for tomorrow's world is a complex process—it takes everyone and the solutions must come from the most exceptional teachers, committed parents, and informed leaders. After all, it is our children that are at stake here. We mothers will not be complacent when it comes to the education of our children—all children!

Since then I have learned two things. The first is that once elected, legislators aren't really held accountable for the decisions they make. In many states they are term limited and so they carry out their service and move on. It takes years to fully understand the true impact of many of these policies, and even then, we spend little time reflecting on the results.

The second thing I learned is that a great many of the mothers out there really are complacent. There are some exceptions, but the rate at which women fail to even vote today is frightening. Who will speak for the children if not their mothers? There can be accountability in government only if there is citizen participation—making good decisions in the voting booth, understanding the challenges and being informed on the issues, exercising our voice and our values, and fully participating in politics at every level. Such citizenry was the bedrock belief of our nation's founders. Accountability—politically, economically, and socially—begins with education. The promise of democracy, economic sustainability, and social progress are realized only through us—the people.

The Great Hoax

The premise of education accountability is like the magician who divides the hapless lady in the box. Eventually, we all learn that those legs extending from the bottom are fakes. The entire reform movement, built on the presumption of accountability, is a similar hoax. It is a trick we have played on ourselves.

I am often asked why we the public have allowed the federal government to play such an intrusive role in our educational system, especially considering that the federal stream of funding is less than 10 percent of school revenues. The answer points decisively to the core of our accountability dilemma. The average American family is preoccupied with the demands of everyday life, burdened by the realities of a perpetually tenuous economy. Bombarded with advertising and political propaganda and overwhelmed by vast amounts of information, we fall victim to the ever-increasing disconnect between citizens and our government. In the end, we have yielded to solutions beyond ourselves, hoping to relinquish responsibility to trustworthy external monitoring systems.

Today's accountability simply defers our obligation to our children and their education to an external outfit. It has been more convenient to monitor our schools with the oversimplistic, irrelevant test scores printed in the newspaper than to become personally involved in education. In the accountability hoax, we ourselves have become the magician smiling as he saws, the contorted woman collaborating in the deception, and the surprised audience gasping in astonishment. The current condition of our schools is a result of our own doing—and our own undoing.

The Purpose of Accountability

True accountability should accomplish three objectives:

- Improve transparency—to help the public know how schools are spending our tax dollars and also what and how our children are learning.
- Prevent fraud and corruption—to identify those who deceive the system and subvert funds intended to improve learning for children.
- Shine the light on problems—to identify weaknesses in individual districts and schools so that problems can be quickly and effectively corrected and the troubled schools made stronger.

Recent trends in school accountability have been primarily driven by business leaders who promote a corporate model. The findings of works such as *Why Is Corporate America Bashing Our Schools?* concur.[1] By adopting the enterprise system, or the total quality management model, or the factory paradigm, or whatever business approach you prefer to call it, five- to eighteen-year-olds enrolled in public schools are on their way to being efficiently streamlined—all under the banner of accountability.

Transparency

Transparency in public schools has indeed improved. We now know what and how our children are learning—by their performance on shallow, multiple-choice questions that have little relevance to the information and processes they will need in an actual democracy, career, or in real life. It's also blatantly clear where our tax dollars are being directed: at complying with government mandates and standardized tests.[2]

Had the federal government not fallen short in meeting the cost demands of fully implementing NCLB, we may have very well succeeded in producing a standardized American workforce. It is difficult to imagine the value of such a feat, as overseas production and standardized labor continue to be available at a fraction of the costs of doing business in the United States.

We have altered the foundation of education in an effort to become more responsive and have lost our way in the process. Had we chosen to become more responsive to the whole child, we could have perhaps made advancements in human development. Had we altered our vision to prepare a twenty-first-century workforce, our professional community may have benefited. Had we intended to produce a powerful citizenry, we would have advanced a sincere democracy. Instead, we chose to reduce learning, achievement, and the complexity of human beings to simple measurable indicators. We chose to transform the function and purpose of our schools from educating children to reporting to government. This is quite a contradiction, considering that the purpose of representative government is to report to its citizenry.

Now here's the real kicker. Whereas public schools have become more transparent, the corporations paid to monitor our schools have no transparency whatsoever. They have become the sole judges of student achievement, teacher quality, and school success, but they are subject to no evaluation or scrutiny. Some state protocols threaten teacher dismissal if they even look at the test they are administering. Parents have no access to their children's actual test responses. The corporations paid with our tax dollars to monitor students and judge schools are completely concealed from public oversight. Can you see the fake legs protruding from the box?

Fraud and Corruption

Now to the magic box itself: the leading driver and key lobbyist behind No Child Left Behind, Sandy Kress, held contracts with McGraw-Hill as he drafted the NCLB bill.[3] Kress was also the architect of the Governor's Reading Initiative in Texas. Eventually, that same model was adopted at the national level. "Reading First" and NCLB landed McGraw-Hill a large share of the nation's textbook market along with the lion's share of the nation's testing market.

Corporate leaders, like those associated with the Business Roundtable, continue to bank on public policy. With the passage of NCLB, billions of tax dollars were directed to test publishers and data managers, including Harold McGraw III, chair of the

Table 3.1 Test Publishers' Profit Increase from 2001 to 2006
(in millions)

	2001	2006	% Increase
McGraw-Hill	$273	$329	20.4%
Pearson	(£432)	£469	210.9%
ETS	$4.2	$7.3	71.9%

Business Roundtable and CEO of McGraw-Hill. In 2000, the year that NCLB was presented to Congress, the Business Roundtable invested $68,104,955 in soft money, political action committees (PACs), and individual campaign contributions. The organization then invested in eighty lobbyists in twenty-one lobbying firms, to the tune of $21,480,000.[4] "Bush signed No Child Left Behind into law in January 2002. Five months later, Kress registered with the U.S. Secretary of the Senate as a lobbyist for NCS Pearson. Kress specializes in helping his clients tailor themselves to the requirements of No Child Left Behind, something Pearson has done with startling success."[5] People often ask me if there is any benefit to NCLB. I say, "You betcha"; just take a look at those profit increases shown in Table 3.1.

For the record, Kress's client list also includes Educational Testing Services (ETS), Kaplan, and HOSTS Learning—online testing and educational services. Look to future policies to benefit corporate online educational services. Education industry leaders, like Kress and Harold McGraw III, have turned lawmaking into moneymaking. According to the National Council of State Legislators, it costs $135 million just to comply with the *reporting* requirements of NCLB.[6]

In today's democracy there are sixty lobbyists for every member of Congress. While our political leaders are elected to represent us, thousands of lobbyists are paid handsomely to represent corporate financial interests. Often times, it's their personal interests that are being represented. We, the people, are simply outnumbered. In this way, recent policies in education aren't any different than policies involving insurance companies, pharmaceutical industries, oil, or homeland security. We just need to follow the money. Then we need to reclaim our federal and state legislatures as institutions for the people.

Today's education reform isn't about outranking other nations, and it isn't about improving learning for our children. The competition that exists today is between test publishers and data management systems competing for financial markets and economic targets—our tax dollars and our children. Perhaps it's best understood in the words of Harold McGraw III, president and CEO of McGraw-Hill Companies and chair of the Business Roundtable: "The key to CTB's base business is the implementation and continued funding of NCLB's assessment and accountability provisions. The current Federal budget allocates $390 million for state development and implementation of these requirements. Most states will supplement their allocations."[7]

The question of who benefits (or should we say, who profits) from standardization and high-stakes testing grows increasingly clearer. Unbeknownst to the masses, control over our nation's public education system and the futures of our children have been slipped into the pockets of private enterprises. Our current accountability system has not only failed to root out fraud and corruption but also has institutionalized them in our children's classrooms.

The Reading First scandal is a primary example. The Education and Labor Committee investigation into the Reading First program revealed that President Bush's advisors broke the law to promote the $6 billion program.[8] The hearings exposed evidence that these same advisors improperly benefited from contracts for textbooks and testing materials they personally designed. A thorough study from the U.S. Education Department's Institute of Education Sciences (IES) determined that children in schools receiving Reading First funding had virtually no better reading skills than those in schools that didn't get the funding.[9]

Many argue that public policy should not be linked to corporate profit margins. That is surely reasonable, given the long history involving corporate misuse of government policies in this country. The problem is not that these companies are getting rich. The problem is that they are getting rich on bad policy. Mark Twain said, "Put all your eggs in one basket and watch that basket." We have not done that. We have transferred our own accountability to educational publishers, whose incentive is improving profits, not improving schools. High-stakes testing and accountability reforms have in fact brought *less* accountability while inspiring ever-increasing opportunities for corporate fraud and corruption.

Identifying Problems and Implementing Solutions

In 2007 *Time* magazine released an evaluation of No Child Left Behind. The authors of the report gave the policy an F in school improvement.[10] Wasn't the whole purpose of NCLB to improve schools?

In a letter to Massachusetts Senator Edward Kennedy, Marion Brady, author of *Max & Me: The Abuse of Power in Florida Community Colleges*, had this to say regarding the reauthorization of NCLB:

> You're misdiagnosing the fundamental problem with American education—a curriculum, adopted in 1892, designed for a tiny minority of students.
>
> By any legitimate measure, that curriculum is failing. But instead of calling for a thorough examination of this taken-for-granted, 115-year-old relic from a by-gone era, your NCLB legislation is freezing it even more rigidly in place. You're beating a near-dead horse. Quality doesn't lie in doing the wrong thing better.[11]

Today's accountability systems have not improved schools or children's learning. In fact, NCLB labels many of the best schools in the country, even blue ribbon schools, as not meeting "adequate yearly progress" (AYP). Schools with high graduation rates, extensive course electives, high teacher retention, and community support are being labeled as "failing schools." All fifty states have been unsuccessful at meeting the criteria of AYP as defined by NCLB. It is becoming quite clear that the failure is not with our schools but with our policies.

Accountability Gone Awry

David Tyack and Larry Cuban concur that reforms "have added complexity, brought incoherence," and "made new demands of time on heavily burdened teachers."[12] According to one survey, 88 percent of superintendents polled assert that "keeping up with all the local, state and federal mandates handed down to the schools takes up way too much time."[13] Competing accountability systems have been proven ineffective and costly. Table 3.2 illustrates today's multiple systems of accountability.

Table 3.2 Conflicting Systems of Accountability

Federal Government	State Government	State Depts. of Education	Locally Elected School Boards	On-site Managers
No Child Left Behind requires all children to be 100% proficient on state standardized tests by 2014.	These vary from state to state, but many states have their own Accountability Mandates, often more severe than NCLB.	State regulating agencies monitor schools and their accreditation, license teachers, and enforce state and federal mandates.	As district regulating bodies, school boards institute local policies and implement student, teacher, and school regulations.	Superintendents, principals, school accountability teams, parents, and students. Evaluate schools, teachers, programs, and provide insight and feedback. Enforce federal, state, and district mandates.

Everyone is talking accountability, but the determination of "who is responsible" or "what for" has yet to be fully answered. The federal government's indicators of quality, NCLB, are quite different from state indicators of quality, which in turn are often different from district indicators of quality, which have become very different from teachers' and parents' values of quality. Today's teachers are spending more time "accounting for their work" than they are working. It's no wonder that the attrition rate for teachers is so high.[14] A teacher must now serve federal mandates, state mandates, licensing and accreditation requirements, his or her local school board, district administrators, the school principal, and parents. The opportunity to serve children is what calls teachers to the education profession, and yet the children are the last to be considered here in "full spectrum accountability."

Conflicting Measurement Tools

Conflicts in accountability systems have created confusion and have absorbed billions of dollars. Federal and state government representatives rely on state standardized tests as the measurement device. Yet the data has shown that state test results do not correlate with national standardized test results. The conflicting data reflects more about the measurement tool than students' abilities.

"In Alabama, for example, 73% of fourth-graders scored at a 'proficient level' on state math tests in 2005, but only 21% were 'proficient' on the National Assessment Educational Progress (NAEP). Among Arizona fourth-graders, 72% were proficient on state reading tests, but only 24% were proficient on NAEP."[15] A report sponsored by the Fordham Institute also identifies major discrepancies in state tests as well as differences in how states interpret and report student success.[16]

A word of caution: the public must approach think-tank reports with a great deal of skepticism. Although the media is quick to report on think-tank findings and solutions, the majority are independently financed and politically motivated. Recently the Education Policy Research Unit at Arizona State University and the Education and the Public Interest Center at the University of Colorado at Boulder together launched the Think Tank Review Project. The purpose of the organization is to provide expert reviews of think-tank reports. In 2006, the first year of the project, thirteen think-tank reports were reviewed. Only two could be considered to have minimally passed expert muster. "For instance, empirical analyses have been shockingly shoddy, and the findings, conclusions, and recommendations have consistently extended beyond those analyses."[17] It is a recent trend for media, policy wonks, and staff development trainers to rely on think tanks in an attempt at "research-based decision making," which may explain the breakdown in school improvements and legitimate policy.

Conflicting Reports

Once collected, conflicting test results are then used to inform the public of something. Unfortunately, there are also variations and vague translations within the required reporting procedures, resulting in the dissemination of a multitude of mixed messages. Parents and community members frequently receive state or district reports that illustrate "successful ratings," followed by additional reports showing national discrepant data and conclusions implying "failure." Managing these four or five redundant and conflicting systems of accountability has created a bureaucratic vacuum of time, money, and talent and contributed to mass confusion.

Values that Matter

One of the biggest problems we have in education right now is that school policies and practices are out of line with our hopes and values for our children. At the beginning of my daughter's third grade school year, several parents came to me with a concern that afternoon recess had been eliminated. The cancellation of recess seems to be the new epidemic in our public schools.[18] According to the National Parent Teacher Association, nearly 40 percent of U.S. schools have either canceled recess or are considering doing so because of budget cuts and the time constraints of standardized testing.[19]

I sat down with the principal and asked, "What will it take to have the afternoon recess reinstated for these eight- and nine-year-old children?" I explained that the American Association of Pediatrics has recommended extended periods of unstructured play and advocated for school recess. I reminded him that the rate of childhood diabetes has tripled over the past twenty years. I shared with him that while schools across the country are shortening or eliminating recess, pediatricians are working to address the epidemic of childhood obesity. I then asked if he was aware that our nearby hospital reported the highest rate of teen suicides in the state.

This situation illustrates the central problem facing parents across this nation. Politicians, lobbyists, school board members, school administrators, and even teachers continue in their efforts to make children fit the policies. The solution is the other way around. Instead of making our children conform to the policies, we need policies that conform to the needs of our children.

I concluded the recess conversation by saying, "I know it's been a long time, but don't you remember recess? Isn't that the reason we didn't drop out in the fourth grade?" Education is not about profit or even performance; it's about children. The social, emotional, physical, intellectual, and nutritional needs of children are at the core of parents' values.

Before teachers were accountable to McGraw-Hill, Pearson, and ETS, they were accountable to citizens, elected school boards, district and school administrators, and parents. And before standards-based education, they were accountable for a lot more than test scores. Those who are calling for an end to high-stakes testing aren't asking for less, we are asking for *more*.

Our wish is for administrators and teachers to be responsible in the areas for which they have control and to focus on goals that actually matter to our kids and teenagers. For example:

- Create a safe and secure environment in order for children to feel comfortable to accept challenges and take risks.
- Provide challenging and meaningful instruction that inspires and motivates children and engenders a sense of personal responsibility for life-long learning.
- Maintain high expectations for every child; acknowledge individual needs and abilities, and build on children's unique talents and strengths.
- Recognize the whole child—physically, emotionally, and intellectually.
- Ensure each child's continued progress and ongoing development.
- Approach instructional content in a way that honors human development, scientific principles, and real-world understanding and that represents effective teaching practices.
- Cultivate respectful relationships that nurture children with firm guidance, honest valuations, and encouragement. Include parents and involve the community.
- Foster an atmosphere of fairness and equity where differences are valued and every child, parent, and colleague is treated with dignity and consideration.
- Be intentional, thoughtful, reflective, and organized.
- Make learning fun for both student and teacher, invite curiosity, stretch each child's potential and imagination, share their dreams, and pay tribute to their very short childhood.
- Provide instructional content and experiences that prepare students for democracy, the workforce, and lives that are both personally fulfilling and contribute to the worldwide community.

You can't measure these qualities. Government can't quantify these types of values, but it is objectives like these that will lead to superior educators, effective schools, and caring intellectuals.

Accountability Realized

Accountability in education doesn't reside in government ideals, artificial controls, or constructed measurement devices. The answers are where they have always been: with the people. The missing keys are not mandates or measurements or business principles. What is missing is trust. Are we going to trust corporate executives and their educational products to ready our children? Are we going to trust government legislators and their mandates to instruct our future? Or are we going to trust administrators and teachers to direct student learning and drive educational decisions?

What's more, are we going to trust parents to be advocates and the disciplinarians of their children? And are we going to trust students on their way to becoming adults to seize educational opportunities for their betterment and ours?

Answer however you wish, but understand that to look for the answers outside of ourselves is to defer responsibility. Human beings are complex, and the challenge of educating a racially, economically, and socially diverse population represents an enormous challenge. We have to abandon the artificial illusions of accountability, change our priorities, and adopt leadership models where the stakeholders share in the responsibility for our public schools and our children.

Let there be no mistake that educators must be the primary decision makers in education. It's time we stop empowering the tests and the school ratings and begin empowering the people who inspire, motivate, and educate our children. So long as the federal government is in the driver's seat of our classrooms, we can expect to see declines in academic quality.

This doesn't mean that the federal and state governments do not play a role in improving our schools. It does mean that the role they play is secondary. Table 3.3 provides an alternative to high-stakes testing and feigned accountability. It's nothing ground-breaking or cutting edge, but it's real, achievable, and offers the kind of improvements that lead to meaningful learning and opportunities for children. In the end we have to trust each other again; there's no other alternative.

Table 3.3 Educational Governance Model

Government	Local	State	Federal
Agency	Elected School Board	State Department of Education	U.S. State Department of Education
	District administrators	Elected State Board members	
	Teachers as leaders Parents as leaders Students as leaders		
Authority	Oversees schools; held accountable by local citizens	Oversees districts; held accountable by citizens of the state and the elected state legislature	Oversees State Departments of Education and is held accountable by the president
Responsibility	Support and monitor students (through a variety of assessments)	License teachers	Collaborate with State Dept. of Education
	Support and monitor teachers (through annual evaluations)	Accredit districts (enforce state statutes and federal laws)	Monitor accreditation agencies
	Support and monitor schools (through school improvement plans)	Network districts and centralize communication to share information and provide for the efficient utilization of resources	Collect and report research findings, case models, and education success stories
		Collect and report research findings, case models, and education success stories	Network State Departments and centralize communication to share information and provide for the efficient utilization of resources

Local Governance

In the local governance model, schools are regulated through public input and oversight. Educators are certified through teacher education programs, licensed by the state, cleared through police background checks, follow district and state curriculum guidelines, and evaluate their students through both informal and formal assessments. Educators are also evaluated annually and are supervised by their administrators who see their primary role as enabling teachers to do what they do best—teach.

Improving Local School Boards

America's affinity for local control dates back to early colonial experiences—for example, Massachusetts, Pennsylvania, and Virginia. As Philip Abbott writes, "Revolution represented the 'birth' of the American Republic, and the formation of colonial settlements represented its gestation."[20] It is our American tradition that the power shall reside in the people. Our public schools must therefore be governed in that same tradition: to uphold the will of the majority while preserving with equal law the rights of the minority. According to the National Civic League, "Communities that deal successfully with the challenges they face have a clear sense of their past and a shared picture of where they want to go. Communities that have a shared vision are more likely to spend their time on the things that truly matter rather than wasting energy on smaller reactive issues."[21] Herein lies the power of local school boards.

There is room, however, to improve the model of local school boards and their effectiveness in governing our nation's schools. Every district and county throughout this nation is called to reflect on the composition of its school board. If we are to make better decisions in education, it is essential that school boards represent their stakeholders. This means that every school board should consist of one school administrator, one teacher, one current parent, one student, and one city or state legislator. Each of these representatives should be elected by the members they represent. For example, teachers elect one teacher, parent associations hold elections for one parent, students elect school representatives for the student council as well as one high-school student to serve on the board, and then include either or both a city council member and state legislator from the same district. Each representative would be responsible for informing his or her stakeholder group about the decision being made by the board as well as for collecting information and input to carry back to the board.

Districts could continue to hold public elections for one or two at-large members elected by the community if they so choose. This composition ensures that everyone who has a stake in education also has a voice in the decision making. It also ensures that those who are in the position of making educational decisions are better informed by the educators and administrators implementing the policies and by the students and parents who are being most impacted by those policies.

Restoring Local Control

This type of reorganization cannot be enacted overnight. Instead, it is a process that would be phased in on a gradual schedule to allow existing elected board members to fulfill their terms. However, with this reconstitution of school boards, teachers, government leaders, students, and parents can exchange information, better coordinate, and greatly improve the decision making process at the local level. Eventually, local school boards can then begin governing again.

Monitoring Students

It is imperative that in any profession the evaluators are the experts, professionally trained and experienced to render accurate and informed judgments. Teachers hold students accountable in a variety of ways, some measurable and some not. Students themselves are motivated differently as well. Some care about grades whereas others are only inspired if the work is worthwhile and personally challenging.

Educational decisions such as program eligibility, matriculation, or graduation should never be determined by a single indicator, such as a test score, but rather by a body of evidence and by those parents and educators with direct insight and oversight of the student. Such materials and factors as teacher evaluations, coursework, review committees, portfolios, behavioral expectations, discipline policies, and involvement in academic, volunteer, and extracurricular experiences should be given consideration in such circumstances.

Assessments should be varied and appropriate. For example, students in a math and science magnet school should be held to different and more suitable expectations for writing. They may never be authors, but they may be great astrophysicists, geologists, or mechanical engineers. A more appropriate assessment for a student in a vocational school may be to rebuild an engine rather than to fill in a bubble. These types of variations do not lend themselves to government tracking but are absolutely necessary for developing the talents of our next generation and for improving instruction and learning for individual students.

Monitoring Teachers

Before tests were the sole measure of a teacher's success, the school principal evaluated teachers. Much like other professions—including engineers, health care professionals, construction workers, journalists, and salespeople—teachers are monitored by their supervisors. In many districts throughout the country, principals are required to observe and evaluate teachers multiple times throughout the year.

Educator evaluation forms need to be collaboratively developed by school board members, administrators, teachers, and parents, with the input of students. Professional objectives must center on the development of the individual educator and should reflect the mission and goals of the particular school.

The evaluation forms themselves should not be standardized, nor should they be based on standardized tests. A Montessori teacher, a physical education teacher, a video production teacher, and an environmental education teacher, for example, should not all be evaluated according to the same criteria. There are, however, some general expectations, and the majority of states have adopted professional teaching standards similar to the following Illinois Professional Teaching standards:

Illinois Professional Teaching Standards

#1 Content Knowledge
The teacher understands the central concepts, methods of inquiry, and structures of the discipline(s) and creates learning experiences that make the content meaningful to all students.

#2 Human Development and Learning
The teacher understands how individuals grow, develop, and learn and provides learning opportunities that support the intellectual, social, and personal development of all students.

#3 Diversity
The teacher understands how students differ in their approaches to learning and creates instructional opportunities that are adapted to diverse learners.

#4 Planning for Instruction
The teacher understands instructional planning and designs instruction based upon knowledge of the discipline, students, the community, and curriculum goals.

#5 Learning Environment
The teacher uses an understanding of individual and group motivation and behavior to create a learning environment that encourages positive social interaction, active engagement in learning, and self-motivation.

#6 Instructional Delivery
The teacher understands and uses a variety of instructional strategies to encourage students' development of critical thinking, problem solving, and performance skills.

#7 Communication
The teacher uses knowledge of effective written, verbal, non-verbal, and visual communication techniques to foster active inquiry, collaboration, and supportive interaction in the classroom.

#8 Assessment
The teacher understands various formal and informal assessment strategies and uses them to support the continuous development of all students.

#9 Collaborative Relationships
The teacher understands the role of the community in education and develops and maintains collaborative relationships with colleagues, parents/guardians, and the community to support student learning and well-being.

#10 Reflection and Professional Growth
The teacher is a reflective practitioner who continually evaluates how choices and actions affect students, parents, and other professionals in the learning community and actively seeks opportunities to grow professionally.

#11 Professional Conduct
The teacher understands education as a profession, maintains standards of professional conduct, and provides leadership to improve student learning and well-being.

It makes sense to incorporate these types of professional teacher objectives into an annual evaluation process. Keep in mind that individual goals are critical for improving one's professional development and that teachers, like students, need the kind of guidance and support that will lead to personal improvement.

Developing Teachers

School board members often recognize the importance of developing high-quality teachers, and they devote the necessary resources to support, advance, and reinforce great educators.[22] Douglas County, Colorado, and other districts employ a Building Resource Teacher (BRT) for each school. The BRTs participate in the formal evaluations process, supervise, and provide ongoing staff development training for teachers.

As a young teacher, I met weekly with my school's BRT to plan lessons, prepare assessments, evaluate students' work, and discuss challenges. In my district, probationary teachers were required to meet for two hours after school every week. During these meetings we received staff development training in classroom management, organization, parent conferences, facilitating reading groups, problem-solving, science, social studies, differentiating and modifying instruction, integrating curriculum, creating and grading assessments, working with learning disabilities and the gifted and talented, and so forth. Whatever skills I brought to the teaching profession were multiplied ten-fold as a result of this extensive modeling and support system.[23] Unfortunately, today's system of accountability has turned teachers into the enemy and pits administrators against the faculties they are designed to support.

Monitoring Schools

The problem with a national accountability system rests in its inability to account for, or address, the specific needs of each district, education board, or community school. The collaborative development of "individual school improvement plans" is an effective alternative, which ensures meaningful accountability. The function of a school improvement plan is to identify current challenges, specific problems, deficiencies in student development, budget restrictions, teaching deficits, and school system flaws. The improvement plan creates solutions specific to that school's challenges and targets available resources accordingly.

In my third year of teaching, a variety of reading assessment tools indicated that our students had, on average, a one-year gap in reading ability between fiction and nonfiction reading assessments. As a result of those findings, our school's annual goal emphasized reading, and we developed a plan to improve students' literacy abilities in nonfiction. Our plan included teacher scholarships for workshops, staff-development seminars, a parent guide for reading nonfiction, budget investments in nonfiction books and magazines for classrooms, a parent/teacher/student after-school book study, and the schoolwide implementation of new nonfiction instructional strategies.

The success of individualized, collaboratively developed school improvement plans was certain because the teachers, students, and parents responsible for implementing the plans understood the need for change and drove the process. Individualized school improvement plans are the best way to ensure that schools are adopting goals specific to their students and their community and that improvement is ongoing. Though such plans don't provide neat comparisons, general ratings, or numeric qualifiers, they do allow for school boards and the public to closely monitor the continual development and effectiveness of each school.

State Governance

State education departments cannot effectively monitor thousands of teachers and millions of children from behind their desks, especially on the basis of single data points. School operations and the oversight of teachers, students, and schools are far more effectively governed by district administrators and locally elected school boards accountable directly to the citizens. The role of state departments of education is most appropriately suited to establishing evaluation schedules and procedures, licensing teachers, enforcing state laws, ensuring that schools are accredited, and monitoring school and district improvement plans.

Licensing Teachers

States are ultimately responsible for ensuring that every teacher is degreed, certified, and licensed and has undergone an extensive background check. Sadly, we are witnessing an inverse trend in this nation. In the era of accountability, and with fewer individuals entering the education profession, states are loosening their licensing standards and issuing provisional teaching licenses to those without the necessary qualifications. Teacher quality is considered by many researchers to be the number-one indicator of a school's success. "Education reformers" contradict themselves by demanding higher expectations and simultaneously weakening teacher guidelines.

In addition to extensive coursework, teaching candidates must first perform a year or more of classroom observation and student teaching before completing their degrees and earning certification. No one should teach in a public school who is not professionally educated, skilled, and licensed in the field of education. States offering "provisional licenses" to those with zero classroom experience and no education coursework are taking a step backward in school improvement and accountability.

Accrediting Schools

In addition to monitoring teacher licenses, state education departments monitor schools through the accreditation process. This is a common practice in every state, though there is some variation between accrediting agencies and protocols. Accrediting schools improves accountability because a nonprofit professional board comprised of researchers, administrators, parents, teachers, and citizens evaluates each school through an in-depth review process.

A body of evidence including formal and informal assessments, parent surveys, educator observations, student and faculty interviews, and reviews of curriculum, course syllabi, discipline procedures, and so forth are all considered in the accreditation process. Accreditation and district improvement plans are yet another way states can improve transparency, prevent against fraud and corruption, and begin solving problems and improving our schools.

Federal Governance

Recent recommendations in the reform debate have suggested the elimination of local school boards and the centralization of power under the federal government in the way of national standards and a national standardized test.[24] Before another cog in the wheel is reinvented, please remember that we already have a national test, the NAEP (National Assessment of Educational Progress). NAEP has been administered to a sample of students in all fifty states, Puerto Rico, and the District of Columbia since 1992. And although national standards have yet to be formalized, state standards have been modeled after national standards such as those developed by the National Council of Teachers of Mathematics (NCTM). We do not necessarily need to rewrite another version of standards. We do need to place the emphasis on supporting faculties, engaging parents and community members, and empowering students.

There has been a general consensus among the public to keep the federal government out of the day-to-day operations of our nation's schools. The rationale is simply that local communities and the citizens of those communities are better equipped and more effective at acknowledging their problems, addressing public concerns, and seizing opportunities.[25] "The most innovative and successful communities in America have at least one thing in common—strong civic infrastructure."[26]

Recent failures illustrate why the federal government and corporate testing companies should not be charged with monitoring the day-to-day operations of the 94,090 schools in our nation's 16,850 school districts. A decentralized approach in educational accountability is more effective and less costly. Although the federal government should not attempt to monitor the details of every neighborhood school, it should ensure that all states meet the following criteria:

- Every classroom is taught by a licensed professional educator.
- Each state meets adequacy requirements for school funding.
- Each state implements an "equity model" that ensures equal opportunity, quality educators, and access to resources for all children in public education.
- Every public school in the nation is accredited.
- Schools actively work to ensure economic and racial tolerance and promote a climate that honors our nation's tradition of diversity.

When President Lyndon Johnson set out to improve America's schools, he launched a war on poverty. When George W. Bush set out to improve our schools, he launched a war on education. The initial 1965 Elementary and Secondary Education Act resulted in the highest college enrollment and employment of women, minorities, and people with disabilities in our nation's history.[27] Under the ruling of *Brown v. Board of Education* and national efforts to desegregate our schools, we experienced an actual narrowing of the achievement gap and lessened real opportunities for poor and minority children to advance.

Repeal No Child Left Behind

No Child Left Behind Act, in contrast, has wasted billions of dollars, increased dropout rates, and diminished schools resources and teachers' effectiveness. Expanding the reach of the federal government into the operations of our neighborhood schools has drawn criticism from Democrats and Republicans alike. Yet, with the exception of a few, most leaders still advocate revisions and reauthorization of the failed act.

NCLB is a fundamentally flawed policy. Despite nearly a decade of standardization, high-stakes testing, and negative outcomes, many continue to argue for new versions of standards and more tests.

We should all agree to national comparisons the moment our children are born identical, with the same opportunities, living in matching communities, with measurably similar families, and attending duplicative schools. Comparisons are irrelevant when the subjects being measured are so widely dissimilar. We are spending our money in the wrong places, and we are spending our time on the wrong objectives. In his article "Why the No Child Left Behind Act Is Unsalvageable," Eric Schaps writes:

> The intentions behind the legislation may be good, but no amount of tweaking will fix several fatal flaws. In part, these flaws are inherent in the law's unrealistic goals, which, because they can't be met, set schools up to fail. And in part, the flaws are inherent in the law's basic strategy for realizing its goals: high-stakes testing. That strategy ignores the primary reasons for the inequities that schools are supposed to redress, and also causes collateral damage of several kinds.[28]

We can try to direct outcomes, regulate individuals, and manipulate the systems. In the end, we will find that whatever we may have gained by the illusion of "control" has meant sacrificing academic and personal integrity. As Don Perl stated, "Human potential cannot be measured, and trying to do so is only a waste of money and folly of enormous, devastating proportions."[29] The only appropriate course of action is to repeal the No Child Left Behind Act.

Unveiling the Hoax

True accountability in education will require that we put down the saw, crawl out of the box, and look beyond the props. Computer-generated tests have not made teachers more accountable. NCLB has not improved our schools. America's capacity for sustained change in our public education system depends upon our civic vitality. As is the design of democracy, we are the magic formula, we are the integrity in the system; we are the answer to accountability.

❧ 4 ❧

Challenges

In 1991 I founded a mentoring and tutoring program for at-risk students in Denver. Daniel had been previously placed with two other volunteers before we found each other. He was eight years old when we first met; today he is twenty-five. Daniel is an exuberant optimist. He's always smiling, and he's good through and through. His parents have been married for nearly thirty years and are salt-of-the-earth kind of folks.

Like so many Americans, Daniel's father suffers from alcoholism. He worked as a roofer until a fall broke both of his arms. Now he finds work sporadically. His mother, a real gem, works as an aid for children with disabilities in a middle school, barely earning above minimum wage. Daniel's family has endured decades of poverty. The four of them, including Daniel's older sister, once lived in a camping trailer for two years.

I have taught Daniel many things—cutting a steak, understanding percentages, ordering at a restaurant, budgeting, interviewing for a job, the various effects of drug usage, and the dangers of sexually transmitted diseases and out-of-wedlock pregnancies. I watched his first middle-school band recital, drove him to baseball try-outs (he didn't make the team), and watched him graduate from high school (the first in his family).

Partly because of Daniel, I withdrew my application to law school and answered the call to teach. I have found education to be a most worthwhile endeavor. Every challenge our nation faces—national security, protecting the environment and our natural resources, promoting economic stability and balanced budgets, ensuring the safety of our impoverished, abused, and neglected children, and caring for the elderly and disabled—leads back to public education.

I first began this book with the question, "Is public education in the United States really failing?" The first cry of failing schools came when the Russians launched Sputnik, and it did not die when Neil Armstrong took those first steps on the moon. Our public education system has undergone several reforms throughout our nation's history. As population increased, new information became available, and leadership changed, our educational system has adjusted. Still, the answer to the above question is, "Yes." If public education as a whole was succeeding, there wouldn't be a need for this book. This chapter not only answers the question of where we are failing America's children but presents ideas on how we can begin succeeding.

Competing in a Larger Fish Pond

Competition is a major theme in the debate over public education. As national borders disappear from the marketplace, the fish pond grows larger and more crowded. The difficulty we face is determining whether competition or cooperation will best ensure improvements in education, future employment opportunities, and stability here and abroad.

We have entered a global world, which means that the borders politically, economically, and socially are beginning to disappear. While America has undergone some technological and political changes, the changes experienced by other countries have been far more extreme. Women in India, Asia, and the Middle East, for example, now have access to educational and economic opportunity. Even Third World countries are beginning to understand the importance public education plays in economic development and political stability. People breaking the shackles of oppression are hungry. They are hungry to work, hungry to earn, and hungry to live. The hungrier you are, the harder and often smarter you work. The challenge to public education and American society in general is that we are educating generations of youth who are not hungry and have not honed the survival instinct. Many of today's youth are not being guided toward an appreciation of our country's history or our future interdependency.

Simultaneously, we are faced with immigration struggles, outsourcing, and offshoring. H-1B visas are granted to immigrants qualifying for high-tech jobs requiring advanced degrees. U.S. companies filed 119,193 applications for the 65,000 H1-B visas awarded for the fiscal year that began in October 2007.

There were so many applications filed that after two days in April, the government cut them off.[1] The irony is that while corporations look internationally to fill employment positions, other countries continue to send their children to learn and work in America.

Millions of jobs also are being outsourced, and the rate of American corporations moving offshore continues to increase. All of this translates to fewer American jobs. As we export American jobs to those with a greater hunger for education and less available opportunities, unemployment here rises and our economy suffers.

Today's reformers have reshaped public schools in the image of an outdated factory model with the singular purpose of work training. Unfortunately, the standardized training our schools have been forced to provide today prepares students for little more than menial labor—the same jobs that are being outsourced to India, South America, and Asia. Today's salaries for our own low-skilled and service jobs remain below the self-sufficiency standard. Factory and service workers can work full-time and still have their families fall below the poverty line; as the middle class disappears, the number of working poor grows.

Cost, rather than competition or educational experience, is generally the primary driver behind a corporation's decision to outsource. As a country, we are failing to promote employment opportunities, sustainable wages, and economic security for coming generations, and we are doing so at our own expense. Government, using taxpayer dollars, is left to pick up the pieces in the areas of health care, bankruptcy, unemployment, and homelessness.

Standardization and the current educational policies contribute to civic apathy and a lack of global understanding. Corporate greed and the industrial model of education are on course for manufacturing a welfare state.

Regardless of the outreach of this book, we Americans will learn the lessons. Deprivation, starvation, and hardship are sure ways to political reform and social change. Previously in our nation's history, these occurrences have been brought on by depressions and wars, and it appears quite clear that a lack of cooperation and misguided attempts to educate our citizenry has us headed in that same general direction. Competitiveness is the by-product of a world-class educational system. We are losing both.

Good for Business,
Bad for Children

The *fear* of losing or falling behind internationally has advanced high-stakes testing and its emphasis on quantifying and measuring. Again the claim today is that the United States is being outpaced by other industrialized nations. Tests such as the NAEP, Third International Mathematics and Science Study (TIMMS-R), and the Program for International Student Assessment (PISA) reach different conclusions about who's winning and in which categories. On March 26, 2006, two apparently contradictory articles appeared in the *Denver Post*. The first article, "Signs America's Scientific Edge Is Slipping," written by John Aloysius Farrell, the paper's Washington bureau chief, read, in part:

> As China and India grow and join Europe, Japan and other high-tech competitors, the U.S. scientific advantage "is going down pretty rapidly and it's going to continue to fall."

The economist Richard Freeman notes that the wolves have not encircled us yet. America, with but 5 percent of the world's population, still employs nearly a third of the planet's researchers and accounts for 40 percent of research and development spending.

The second article was titled "Too Much Math and Science Make India and Zhou Dull Kids" and was written by Thomas Friedman, author of the best-selling book *The World Is Flat*. Friedman reports on his experiences in Mumbai, India, where he attended the annual meeting of India's high-tech association, Nasscom.

Friedman notes that very few global products have been spawned by India or China. Innovation is often a synthesis of art and science, and the best innovators often combine the two. "We need to encourage more incubation of ideas to make innovation a national initiative," said Azim Premji, the chairman of Wipro, one of India's premier technology companies.

"If we do not allow our students to ask why, but just keep on telling them how, then we are only going to get the transactional type of outsourcing, not the high-end things that require complex interactions and judgment to understand another person's needs," said Nirmala Sankaran, CEO of HeyMath, an Indian-based education company.

It is clear that while Americans emphasize test taking so as not to be "out-engineered," India is working to infuse creativity, divergent ways of thinking, and imagination to spur innovation and invention.

Richard Florida, author of *The Rise of the Creative Class*, argues that the key dimension of economic competitiveness is the ability to attract, cultivate, and mobilize creativity. "Economic growth is a complex process. For most of human history, wealth came from a place's endowment of natural resources, like fertile soil or raw materials. But today, the key resource, creative people, is highly mobile."[2]

Privatization

A great deal of the conservative approach to education points to privatization. The members of the Business Roundtable are anxious for us to turn over our children and hard-earned tax dollars to the corporate leaders of America. Their argument implies that because "government" education has failed, the free market should have a shot at it. Given our nation's history of stock market crashes, recessions, and recurring instances of corporate fraud and corruption, it's clear that the free market hasn't fared so well, either. As a matter of fact, with the 2009 federal bailout, it is our children and their financial futures that have come to the rescue of free market. The only "economic stimulus plan" is education. This country can no longer afford to subsidize CEOs and simultaneously neglect crumbling schools.

The reality is that privatization poses a serious threat to our children, their education, and our future. Fortunately, we don't have to examine models for privatization in hypothetical terms, as there are several current and applicable examples. The most recent and relevant privatization experiments in education have been provided by Chris Whittle, founder and former president of Edison Schools Inc., a for-profit company.

Backed by voucher supporters and powerful conservatives, Edison schools were heralded as the salvation of public education—passing off our accountability once again, through the privatization of neighborhood schools. Edison Schools Inc. claimed it could improve student achievement, run public schools for less money, and return a profit for its shareholders. "Better, cheaper, profitable" became the new motto for educating our children.

Once again, the claims of improving student achievement didn't hold up under scrutiny. Performance outcomes were mixed at best.[3] According to the districts that contracted with Edison, the targeted for-profit schools ultimately cost more to run than public schools. The notion of corporate profits likewise collapsed, as the enterprise lost millions each year. The Edison schools reported a profit in just one quarter during the ten years their financial records were made public. To date, twenty-six schools have cancelled their contracts with Edison Schools Inc., and since May 1, 2002, ten shareholders have filed lawsuits against the corporation.[4] Edison was recently bought out and has moved out of the school management business into the (surprise!) more profitable testing and tutoring industry.

Also noteworthy in the privatization debate is the Pennsylvania case of juveniles being wrongly sentenced to private detention centers. Over a five-year period ending in 2008, PA Child Care and Western PA Child Care paid judges Mark Ciavarella and Michael T. Conahan $2.6 million in kickbacks for closing down a county juvenile detention center and sentencing juveniles to their private facilities. "Judge Ciavarella said he did not sentence juveniles who did not deserve the punishment, but the numbers suggest a different story: he sent one in four of the juvenile defendants to the private detention centers from 2002 to 2006 while the rate elsewhere in the state was 1 in 10."[5] Both judges were charged with wire fraud and conspiracy and sentenced to federal prison.

The principles of profit and competition characterized by privatization models fail when applied to our collective goals for the educational advancement of our citizenry, workforce, and civilization. Public education and child protective services will never be profitable. They are a public service and an essential component of democracy, a thriving economy, and the well-being of our children.

The Merits of Merit Pay

The concept of merit pay, also referred to as performance pay, is based primarily on the value of competition. What the promoters of merit pay fail to recognize is that teachers are already being compensated according to a merit system. Teacher's salaries are calculated according to the merits of education credits and years of experience.

The business community is constantly pushing for performance pay models based on measurable outcomes. In their world, competition and the big bucks are the incentive. Educators don't go into teaching careers for the financial rewards, and we recognize that most important outcomes happen over the long-term.[6] Let's face it; if teachers were economically motivated they would take jobs as bartenders, hair stylists, and sales representatives.

My husband works in the defense industry, and his salary comes from a government contract, very much like teachers. He began his career earning close to the same salary as my teaching salary. Twenty years later, his salary has multiplied five times. He still has another twenty years to work.

In that same time, the salary for a teacher has only doubled, and according to the current salary schedule, has a lifetime cap of three times the starting salary. Both of us have master's degrees, both of our jobs support national goals, and both jobs are paid by you, the taxpayers. If we want to strengthen education and fields like math and science, then we had better begin with marketable salaries and helpful working conditions for teachers.

In terms of performance pay, reformers are now advocating for salaries that are linked to test scores—a most disturbing trend. I first began teaching in a suburban school in one of Colorado's wealthiest school districts. My students were from high-income families, with educated parents. Test scores were high.

Five years later I moved to an inner-city school. By then I had five years of teaching experience, more education, and more confidence. By all indicators I was a better teacher. My students, however, came from the poorest area of town, few of their parents had even a high-school diploma, and they were predominantly minorities. We accomplished great things in my classroom, and yet test scores were low.

According to proposed performance pay models, I would earn more in a wealthy district with students of high socioeconomic status than I would earn teaching children of lesser means. To compensate educators, who are driven to work in impoverished classrooms among violence, in dilapidated school houses, and with inadequate resources, with lower pay because of lower test scores is criminal. Although teaching is a reward in itself, educators still have children to feed, electrical bills to pay, and mortgages to cover.

Merit pay is ineffective for two reasons. First, the merit pay model reinforces the industrial paradigm we have long since outgrown. Take, for example, consumer ratings: each year various automobiles "earn" the top ratings, and yet we don't see every American driving that same car. Our own personal experiences and preferences designate our values and our choices. Unlike cars, each educator is unique and has different strengths and abilities. Administrators, parents, and students all have their favorites, and their reasons differ. No merit system can ever accurately quantify the various aspects that culminate in knowledgeable and inspiring teachers. Efforts to do so have had the same effect as standardization: reinforcing mediocrity.

Second, merit pay relies on numeric measurement devices designed for purposes altogether different than the quantifying of a teacher's effectiveness. Standardized tests are designed for the specific purpose of measuring student responses and can't begin to reflect our exceptional educators or their extraordinary methods of instruction. All labels, criteria, and categories of a teacher's impact are costly, grossly simplistic, and inaccurate. The system's failure to appreciate uniquely brilliant and inspiring teachers is the reason so many of my colleagues have left or been pushed out of the classroom.

Reformers who are looking for a way to attract and retain high-quality teachers need to first look at their attitudes toward those who commit to the education profession. Once the most respected field in our culture, teachers are now condemned and ridiculed by journalists, business leaders, politicians, and destructive school climates. Punishments and sanctions have replaced earlier support systems. Harvard scholar Rogier Gregoire describes the current paradox for today's teachers: "Today a teacher's fondest and most cherished ambitions about themselves and their students are being destroyed by the educational system we once embraced."[7]

Teachers' reward is watching children progress, seeing them learn and accomplish something meaningful. They don't have time for political popularity contests, but they do need professional autonomy and a salary that will support their families.

A Word About Teachers' Unions

I grew up with a detached awareness of the labor movement. My paternal grandfather was a foreman for the Colorado Fuel and Iron steel mill in Pueblo, Colorado. My maternal great-grandfather gave his life to that same steel mill, crushed in the pit by an inexperienced and untrained crane operator. Carlo DeSalvo left behind my grandmother, her nine siblings, and my great-grandmother. During the time before the labor movement, workers had no rights and were subject to dangerous conditions, discretionary employment practices, and arbitrary wage cuts.

Much like business members who join their chambers of commerce, the value of a union is that our united workers have the opportunity for representation and a voice in the decision-making.[8] The bottom line is that there is power in numbers. Yet, just as some corporate leaders abuse their power and authority, we now see that some union administrators do the same.

As standard practice, every union member should request an annual position statement. Unions are held accountable by their members. It is the responsibility of every union member to know which state legislation and city policies are being supported and opposed. It is far easier for union members to replace poor leaders and ineffective lobbyists than it is for employees to replace their corporate executives and company attorneys.

The problems often arise when there is an imbalance of power. When control is concentrated too greatly on a side unwilling to sacrifice or work collaboratively, agreements between workers and executives can become tenuous. We see it today, with corporate CEOs who will transfer jobs to Malaysia before risking a 5 percent personal cut in their multimillion-dollar salaries. We also see it in unions with rigid and overly complex employment policies fashioned in response to power struggles more than to the interests of teachers or children. Some labor agreements have become too complicated and too expensive to maintain and also undermine the very members they are supposed to represent.[9]

The danger is that school budgets are growing smaller while children's needs are becoming greater. The explosion of autism and mental health diagnoses are just two examples. Many superintendents, if permitted, would likely replace experienced master teachers with new, cheaper instructors. Good for budgets—bad for children.

Still, principals and superintendents should be granted the authority to make hiring decisions. If they don't have the power to shape their faculty, then the concept of school leadership is simply an illusion.

Today's collective bargaining agreements essentially assure due process for nonprobationary teachers. Probationary teachers may be fired or have their contracts arbitrarily dropped without explanation. Probationary periods differ from state to state and range from one to three years. This represents one of the longest probationary periods of any profession.

Nonprobationary teachers must be provided with a written justification concerning their loss of position and in many cases can activate an appeal process. These provisions are reasonable and ensure that teachers are not fired over trivial or unjustified matters—for example, if a parent doesn't accept that her child's toy unicorn was confiscated during class (as happened to me!), or if a new school board mandates that creationism should replace the science unit (remember Kansas).

It's a myth that nonprobationary teachers can't be fired. It happens all the time. Moreover, tenure was designed to protect intellectual freedom and uncensored speech—necessities to institutions of learning and democracy.

I recently published an editorial on high-stakes testing in a local newspaper. The following week, a staff columnist provided a rebuttal calling me names and accusing me of being a teachers' union mouthpiece.[10] I don't have any association to teachers' unions—I'm far too contentious. What frustrates me is that each time the topic of education is presented; I inevitably hear the words, "If it weren't for those damn teachers' unions. . . . "

The argument has proven effective in placing blame while shutting down legitimate discussion. If anything, our teachers and their representative organizations may be accused of being too weak rather than too powerful. Teachers today have more responsibility and less authority. The NEA has proven impotent at stopping NCLB, and to date, it hasn't even mustered the courage to call for its repeal. Although I remain a member of the National Parent Teacher Association (PTA), the issues it is busied with are inconsequential to the challenges our children face today.

We must recognize that membership organizations, good or bad, cannot replace personal leadership and an informed and engaged citizenry. *Here we are full circle and back to the purpose of public education.* Although there is room for improvement, if teachers were compensated justly, treated with greater respect, and empowered to improve learning and the lives of the children they serve, collective bargaining wouldn't be such a bone of contention. Annual evaluations and timely intervention plans accompanied by guidance and support offer the potential for new and innovative labor contracts.

However, if the current teachers' unions and parent organizations don't adopt the bold action necessary to protect public education or provide for our children, it's time we as members begin aligning ourselves with the organizations and the individuals that will. I have come to believe that if teachers and parents don't speak up, the profession and the future of our children will be lost.

The Challenge of Compulsory Education

There are those who say, "My children are grown, or I homeschool my own children, so why should I have to pay for other people's children to be educated?" Let me be clear on this point. We have compulsory education funded by the general tax base because democracy requires an educated citizenry, our economy is strengthened by high employment rates, and you are safer with children in schools rather than on the streets. Please visit a Third World country for a living example of the value of compulsory education.

Schools know how to teach division, punctuation, and the scientific method. In all this time and throughout all of these debates, this nation has not found a way for public education to ameliorate the challenges of poverty, neglect, abuse, mental illness, addiction, intolerance, and violence experienced by millions of America's children.

I have taught some of the most wounded children coming out of the worst circumstances. At times, I have cradled them in my arms, and at other times I have blocked their way from leaving my classroom. I have cried with them, and I have scolded them. In this regard, I am not unusual.

Yet, schools don't hold all the keys, and teachers can't do it all. Children need positive environments, strong role models, and the opportunity for parents to earn a living wage so that families can have a better chance at healing themselves.

Business does play a role in American education. Schools educate students, businesses hire them as adults, and those adults go on to earn the wages that support their families and fund the taxes to educate the next generation. This is the cycle. Public schools have the responsibility of promoting individuals who are critical thinkers and self-aware, ambitious, and responsible.

Businesses have the responsibility of hiring these individuals for the work they need done and paying wages that promote self-reliance and opportunities for families to be self-sustaining. Government has the responsibility to direct tax dollars to the public schools and to protect public policies from fraudulent and corrupt business practices. Schools, government, and businesses have the responsibility to work collectively and collaboratively on behalf of our nation's children.

The Biggest Challenge—Poverty

The growing rate of poverty, incarceration, addiction, and mental illness is a strong indication that our nation is failing its children. The 1965 Elementary and Secondary Education Act was initially designed to remove barriers to opportunity for low-income, disabled, and English-second-language (ESL) learners. The results of more dollars targeted to at-risk children were evident: more women, minorities, disabled, and low-income students earning college degrees and contributing to society. Public schools, along with desegregation, IDEA, and the influx of federal dollars in the 1960s and 1970s were equalizing opportunity, improving lives, and strengthening our economy. Unfortunately, the triumph in our nation's social conscience was short lived.

The No Child Left Behind Act redirected funds toward testing and sanctioning schools—resources previously targeted to children in need.[11] New barriers in the form of exit exams have been erected, limiting the opportunities for poor and minority children as well as for children with unique abilities.[12] Modern reforms in education reinforce and in many cases widen the economic divide between the very wealthiest and poorest children.[13]

Today in the United States at the beginning of the twenty-first century we have once again condemned our most vulnerable children. Statistics on children and poverty gathered in 2005 attest:

- The official poverty rate is 12.6 percent of the population.
- 12.9 million children under age eighteen are living in poverty.
- The number of children being born into poverty in the United States is increasing.[14]

In 2007 some 37 million Americans lived below the official poverty line, defined as $19,350 per year for a family of four.[15] A single mother and child are only included in the poverty rate if the mother's income is below $13,896. Millions of children not included in these statistics are barely surviving although they are above the official poverty line.

The reasons are obvious. Children who lack financial resources also lack educational resources. An upper-income child is likely to have two or three years of preschool before entering kindergarten. A recent study confirmed that socialization is primary to successfully educating preschoolers.[16] Children of high socioeconomic status often have their education supplemented with music lessons, sports activities, and cultural alternatives. Their experiences include travel, visits to museums, plays, concerts, and other events. Their rooms are likely cluttered with books, art supplies, and puzzles. It is common for most middle-income children to have access to a computer.

Children of low income, in contrast, do not receive private lessons or sports activities because their parents cannot afford them. They do not have computers or the technology that provides access to information. A child living in poverty is fortunate to receive even one year of Head Start, a program that began in 1965 and was developed to meet the emotional, social, health, nutritional, and psychological needs of disadvantaged preschool children.

The federal government in 2006 decreased funding to the Head Start program by more than $57 million while enrollment increased by 2,208.[17] Research has shown that preschool improves a child's development and positively impacts student achievement for poor and minority children. Currently the

United States provides preschool for only about 60 percent of eligible three- and four-year-olds.[18]

Confronting Realities

As I mentioned earlier, after years of teaching in a wealthy suburb, I transferred to an impoverished inner-city alternative high school. During my first month there, I was called terrible names, threatened with violence, and harassed. So many school critics point to these kinds of incidents and call for greater discipline and more severe punishments. My students didn't lack respect for me, they lacked respect for themselves. I countered their behavior by offering something of value to them and demonstrating respect for myself and for each one of them.

Children faced with poverty, neglect, and violence quickly fall behind in the traditional educational system. On average, my sophomores did the equivalent work of my suburban fifth and sixth graders. I quickly modified the curriculum to prepare them with essential life skills to keep them in jobs, out of jail, out of debt, and alive.

When it came to teaching my students about money I listed five decimal numbers on the board (.01, .10, .001, 1.0, and .100). I asked them to write down the decimal number with the largest value on a piece of paper in pen and turn it over. As I went around to each desk, I began handing out the equivalent value in pennies, dimes, and dollars to what they had written. A look of panic quickly spread throughout the classroom. That was the week my tenth-grade students learned how to add, subtract, divide, and multiply decimal numbers and balance their expenses with their revenues; I was out $4.67.

Teachers cannot eliminate the poverty, violence, neglect, and drug abuse too common in our society, but they can provide a refuge and an alternative. For six to seven hours a day, our children have the opportunities offered by a nurturing school environment where it is safe for them to take risks, lunchrooms that provide warm and nutritious meals, teachers who help them find the best in themselves, and playmates whose giggles provide a glimpse of joy and childhood. It is possible. There are schools across the nation that embody this picture.

However, as national goals for "proficiency," an overreliance on numbers, and an obsession with artificially constructed comparisons replace the goals of developing the whole child, the number of these schools is becoming fewer. Test comparisons and expectations such as "All children will perform at grade level" trivialize a child's learning and a child's life.

Classrooms become places of discouragement, reinforcing the sense of failure many impoverished children experience at home. Government bureaucracy has taken us further away from the child-centered approach necessary for guiding educational decisions and preparing our children with the wisdom, confidence, and abilities needed to overcome conditions of poverty and trauma. A classroom sanctuary where hope and joy is abundant is still our best defense against the hopelessness and despair associated with poverty, neglect, and abuse. We could provide for the intellectual, social, physical, nutritional, and psychological well-being of America's children if doing so were a national priority.

For those less moved by the realities of educating our children at risk, consider a recent report that stated, "Children who grow up poor cost the economy $500 billion a year because they are less productive, earn less money, commit more crimes, and have more health related expenses.[19] We have every reason to address the greatest barriers to student achievement—poverty, abuse, neglect, isolation, and mental illness. What is the phrase school critics are always tossing around? "There are no excuses."

Color-Blind or Blind to Color?

Racism is a most uncomfortable topic. We are confronted daily with generalizations, ugly stereotypes, and decades of learned bias. Bigotry is woven into our social fabric, our economic institutions, and our political policies. We deny, ignore, and justify this part of ourselves because we are ashamed.

Schools in the United States are funded largely by property taxes. Children living in the most expensive homes therefore attend the wealthiest schools; children living in the poorest neighborhoods attend the poorest schools.

On May 17, 2000, forty-six years after *Brown v. Board of Education* was decided, a class action lawsuit, *Williams v. State of California,* was filed on behalf of California's low-income students of color.[20] The case had two main arguments: (1) the state of California has to provide all students the basic resources they need to learn: qualified teachers, enough materials, and decent facilities; and (2) all students have a fundamental right to an equal education. The state of California agreed to settle the case in 2004. Several other states have since faced similar adequacy lawsuits in an effort to make state governments address some of the inequities in our public education system.

Funding disparities continue between districts and within districts. So far, we've attempted equality in access. Every child in this country is guaranteed access to an education. It's by no means an *equal* education, though the idea of access has allowed us some distance from such distinctions.

Since the compulsory schooling decision, children of lesser means have attended schools with less qualified or experienced teachers, fewer resources, and fewer opportunities. Into this paradigm of the past, we appear suddenly determined to advance in the new millennium with equality in expectations. Every child is now expected to earn the same scores, on the same tests, at the same time—by 2014. When will we be prepared to commit to *equality in opportunity*?

In a *Yale Law Journal* article titled "National Citizenship and Equality of Educational Opportunity," Goodwin Liu makes the constitutional argument for equal funding in education. According to Liu and others, the Fourteenth Amendment guarantee for national citizenship requires congressional action to narrow interstate disparities in public education and to revoke the policies that perpetuate interstate inequality.

> Although disparities in educational opportunity still exist within and between school districts in each state, disparities across states are more severe. Adjusting for geographic cost differences and student needs, the ten highest-spending states on average spend over fifty percent more per pupil than the ten lowest-spending states. Low spending states are found in the South, Southwest, and Far West, while high-spending states are clustered in the Northeast, mid-Atlantic region, and Midwest. This geographic pattern reflects the historically uneven development of public education in the United States.[21]

Title I of the Elementary and Secondary Education Act has been criticized by Liu, given its promotion of inequalities by allocating aid in proportion to each state's level of per-pupil spending. "Massachusetts, a wealthy high-spending state, received almost 80% more Title I aid in 2001 than Oklahoma, a poor low-spending state, even though Massachusetts had fewer poor children."[22] Liu offers three solutions toward realizing the Fourteenth Amendment's constitutional promise of equal citizenship. His conclusions involve reforming Title I, allocating aid based on child poverty and adjusted to regional cost differences, without proportion to each state's own per-pupil spending.

In addition to our constitutional obligation, some argue we have a moral responsibility to correct the disparities in our educational system. Edwin Feulner, president of the Heritage Foundation, states, "[America has a] shared moral order that respects human dignity, inculcates decency, overcomes fear, and inspires people to help one another in times of trouble. We have learned truths through the ages, among them that all individuals seek freedom, that human life has intrinsic value, and that it is unjust to show arbitrary preference for some people over others."[23] The American principle "to establish justice" has yet to be realized in American education.

New York Senator Chuck Schumer recommends that we discard the land-based formula for funding public schools altogether.[24] If our commitment is to inclusion, as the "No Child Left Behind" title would suggest, NCLB will have to be replaced with a national directive for adequacy and equality in every school in the nation.

Well, money spent on the wrong objectives doesn't help children. But money spent on the right objectives does. One study of Massachusetts court-ordered education finance reforms found that new state revenues were directed at the lowest-spending districts for which they were intended. The results also clearly indicated that 79 percent of the spending was directed toward capital expenditures or the direct, instruction-related interactions of students and teachers. The success of the 1993 finance reforms were closely linked to local involvement and the fact that in the absence of state-level regulations, resource allocation decisions were made effectively by parents, teachers, and principals.[25]

Separate Is Still Not Equal

It is also notable that the poorest schools in the nation serve predominantly Latino and African American children.[26] Segregation did not die with a Supreme Court ruling.[27] Research shows that America is growing as segregated as in the days before the civil rights movement began.

Whereas the student body in the top third of states in terms of adjusted spending is 70 percent white, 14 percent poor, and 4 percent limited in English proficiency (LEP), the student body in the bottom third of educational spending is less than 50 percent white, more than 18 percent poor, and more than 13 percent LEP. In short, children with the greatest educational needs live disproportionately in states with the lowest education spending.[28]

According to the Civil Rights Project at Harvard University, whites made up 58 percent of the nation's public school enrollment in 2003, but the average white student attended a school that was nearly 80 percent white. African Americans accounted for 17 percent of all students, but the average black student attended a school that was 53 percent black. Latinos made up 19 percent of enrollment but attended schools that were typically 55 percent Latino.[29]

In the 2007 Supreme Court case *Parents Involved in Community Schools v. Seattle School District No. 1*, 05–908, the justices condemned race-based enrollment in a 5–4 decision. The ruling overturned lower-court decisions in the Seattle and Louisville districts' desegregation programs.

Fifty-four years after *Brown v. Topeka Board of Education*, white parents sued on the basis that race-based enrollment was unconstitutional. Justice Anthony Kennedy wrote that school districts "must seek alternatives to the classification and differential treatment of individuals by race." "Differential treatment" is not the problem; "unjust treatment" is. Though we can disagree with the ruling, a new precedent has been set. Justice Kennedy has provided us a new opportunity in which to challenge the federal No Child Left Behind Act, which specifically classifies individual students according to race.

The fact that NCLB categorizes children by race and responds with sanctions and punishments rather than support and resources is an indication of racial and class prejudice. The goals of NCLB were never to support minorities and low-income children as the title would suggest. The drafters of the bill did not intend to create equity or opportunity.[30] Lobbyists and various corporate officials masterfully created a federal mandate with a great title that instituted biased educational policy legitimizing discrimination of children on the basis of race, class, and ability. NCLB and the recent Supreme Court ruling return this country to 1896 and the *Plessy v. Ferguson* Supreme Court ruling—which created legal justification for racial separation on Louisiana rail cars and affirmed a nation's bigotry. High stakes testing and standardization has replaced the back of the bus with the back of the classroom.

We can deliver a man to the moon, transfer millions of dollars online, transplant hearts, and travel to the depths of the ocean floor, but we have not given children of color or little financial means the same education as their middle-class white counterparts. We criticize other nations for their caste systems, but one need only look in our ghettos, our barrios, and our classrooms to see that we are no better, and arguably have less of an excuse.

Teaching Them to Fish

There's no question that our dollars need to be targeted, administered efficiently, and disbursed with long-term goals in mind. Research shows that both the school environment and the social-economic conditions confronting students outside school impact student achievement.[31] For *all* of the children of this nation to be successful, they will need more than good schools. The effects of poor prenatal care, lack of proper nutrition, and exposure to drug abuse and violence continue to have devastating effects on our 13 million children living in poverty and the millions more living above it. Children need safe communities, access to quality health care, nutritious meals, a secure home, stable families, and opportunities to learn. It's a tall order and a necessary one.

Unfortunately, the United States continues to dedicate a lesser percentage of the gross domestic product (GDP) toward the care of children than other leading industrialized nations (see Figure 4.1).[32]

Countries such as Finland have more to show for their investment in their children's education. Out of forty nations participating in the 2003 Program of International Student Assessment,[33] Finland with 580,000 students ranked at the very top in the categories of reading and science, second in math, and third in problem solving. According to the same PISA criteria, U.S. students who were assessed ranked eighteenth overall

Figure 4.1 Social Expenditures as a Percentage of GDP and Child Poverty in the OECD

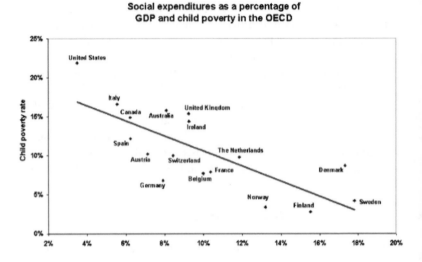

Social expenditures as a percentage of
GDP and child poverty in the OECD

in reading, twenty-second in science, twenty-eighth in math, and twenty-ninth in problem solving. It is also worthy to note that Finland has the fewest days in which students are required to attend school, no standardized testing, professional autonomy, and one of the strongest teachers' unions in the world.

The declining rankings of U.S. students on international test scores, swelling dropout rates, increased youth incarcerations, increases in childhood poverty, and the widening achievement and economic gaps are not the products of failing schools or failing school boards, they are the product of failing priorities. The Nordic countries that outpace the United States in national test scores are the same provinces outpacing us in educational investment. Sweden, Norway, Finland, and Greenland dedicate a greater percentage of resources to educating their citizenry. Their human services and educational systems demand far less, considering their more homogenous population and significantly fewer people living in poverty. Yet these countries invest more of their resources. Here in America we invest less where there is more of a need.

High per-capita income and high productivity make it possible for the United States to afford much greater social spending;

instead we rank the lowest, with about 4 percent of our GDP allocated for social expenditures. Other Organization for Economic Cooperation and Development (OECD) countries "that spend more on both poverty reduction and family-friendly policies have done so while maintaining competitive rates of productivity and income growth."[34] Michael Petit, president and founder of Every Child Matters, explains,

> In contrast, the social programs pushed through by Presidents Roosevelt, Truman, and Johnson, in particular, alleviated widespread poverty among the elderly and were instrumental in creating the nation's great middle class. The actions of these progressive leaders helped enact civil rights laws to end discrimination, provided pensions and health care for tens of millions, sent GI's to college after WWII, and allowed millions of citizens to buy their first homes. For decades, federal laws were enacted to make the workplace safer, control predatory lending, give disadvantaged children a head start, eradicate most of the major communicable diseases, and alleviate hunger. The federal government financed these programs mainly with balanced budgets paid for by taxes that were levied based on a citizen's ability to pay.[35]

Whereas some have argued that social programs are costly and inefficient, Peter H. Lindert, in his book *Growing Public*, has documented the positive correlation of social spending with economic growth since the eighteenth century. Corporate bailouts and decisions to cut taxes for the wealthiest Americans while simultaneously divesting in federal children's health and social programs have produced devastating consequences economically and morally.[36]

Attending to the needs of children takes money. Of course, it will cost even more if we don't invest the money early and in ways that make a difference for children. We can afford it. Consider these national expenditures:

Total child welfare protection expenditures	$22,156,246,128
Total consumer spending on alcohol	$116,000,000,000
Total consumer spending on spectator recreation	$34,800,000,000
Total consumer spending on tobacco	$88,200,000,000[37]

The continued neglect of our schools and our children increasingly perpetuates government dependency. Those students denied educational opportunities are at the greatest risk to become dependent adults, exacting costs to the taxpayer tenfold in the long run. Prisons and unemployment compensation are substantially more expensive than the cost of providing quality public education to all children.

Clearly, other countries have recognized the returns of public education. As those nations address global competition with an educated citizenry, the United States devotes a far greater percentage of resources toward military arsenals, prison systems, standardized tests, and lobbied corporate interests. To the question, "Should we provide for the health and well-being of all children?" today's America has answered with a resounding "NO."

Solutions to the Challenges

Our country has accomplished great things: the defeat of Hitler, the Hoover Dam, the Panama Canal, space travel, cures for life-threatening diseases, and advancements in technology and communications. Surely we can reconcile the inequities in our educational system.

We do not live on islands separate from one another. We are connected and we share interdependence and an uncertain future. If public education is to succeed, if our nation is to succeed, we need to focus on solutions that target resources. We must work to close the racial and socioeconomic discrepancies in our educational system and give all children the opportunity to maximize their full potential and ability to contribute.

It's time to quit *counting* our most vulnerable children and start *helping* them. We may spend twelve years properly educating America's future leaders or the next century making up for it. Their failure is our failure. Their success is our success.

⮞ 5 ⮜

Choices, Choices, Choices

I was surprised what a critic I became when it came to entering my daughter Grace into the world of academia. The journey began when she was just three years old and my search for a worthy preschool ensued. I started by collecting literature on fourteen different preschools (overkill, I know). At last the search was narrowed to four, and I proceeded to set up on-site visits and teacher interviews. I would no more trust a government label on a school than I would take a telemarketer's advice on financial planning.

The first preschool was relatively traditional. I watched as all the children gathered around for storytime and otherwise engaged in their usual sorts of play. I recall the class as consisting of over twenty children and one very young, newly licensed teacher looking a bit overwhelmed.

The second preschool offered a much more progressive environment. The preschool was a fully integrated cultural arts program. In addition to the usual activities, students took special classes in dance, theater, art, and music. I was excited about this program and the opportunity to expose Grace to a variety of creative experiences. Unfortunately, the school environment didn't meet my expectations. The classroom was housed in the local recreation center, and the room was bare. The newly conceived program was still in a developmental stage, not nearly established enough for my preference.

The third preschool was virtually state-of-the-art. The facility was incredible, with large trees, multiple sorts of playground equipment, and picnic tables. The main facility was divided by age groups surrounding a common auditorium and included colorful murals, new carpeting, and a variety of toys and learning materials.

The director was very professional and answered all of my questions concerning what my child would be accomplishing at the school, including letter recognition, one-to-one correlation, and so forth. I watched as the teachers worked with groups of eight children. One group was sorting manipulatives and completing puzzles, another group was neatly seated in red aprons painting a picture, a third group was at play in the kitchen, and others crawled though large plastic tubes mounted on the ceiling. At first, I thought that this was the place for Grace, but at the same time I found something strangely unsettling about the preschool. I added my name to the waiting list anyway.

My last visit was to the oldest licensed preschool in Colorado, St. Timothy's, renamed Wilder Parent Participation Preschool in 2000. When I pulled up to this quiet little church, I wasn't sure where to find the preschool. I nearly got back in my car before noticing an old cement staircase leading to a basement. I descended the stairs, against my better judgment, and opened the door to the sound of children's laughter. Tiny little hands clapped together as a boy dressed in cowboy hat and western vest giddy-upped on a brown pony he had assembled himself. The record player (I didn't even know they still had those) featured a song from somewhere back in earlier eras. There was a separate room just for the blocks, and children were making plans together and building towers. A dove, some fish, a hamster, and two frogs added to the menagerie. The joy in this place was overwhelming.

Wilder offers a community participation preschool, meaning that parents are required to volunteer every third week in the classroom and to play an integral role in the implementation of the day-to-day operations. It has a board and committees, and decisions are made jointly between parents, teachers, and school administrators. Children's art covered every inch of every space, and even though it was noisy and full of all kinds of stuff, there was order and a structure to the place.

I asked a tall women in an apron the usual question: "What sets this preschool apart from the others?" Mrs. Peterson smiled and said with a soft southern accent, "Oh, I don't know about other preschools, but here we honor the natural development of each child, and we believe that learning is done through play and interactions with the world. We provide a safe, nurturing environment where children are introduced to many experiences and opportunities to laugh, explore, take risks, share, and ask questions—the usual kid stuff."

Instantly I realized what was missing from the manicured

classrooms and well-groomed pupils at the preschools I had visited earlier; it was the chatter of children. There was little interaction between the children in their orderly groups, and I don't
recall seeing one smile or hearing the sound of laughter.

I'm certain if Grace had attended the state-of-the-art preschool, she would have graduated to kindergarten counting further, reciting the correct combinations of colors, and perhaps
even reading. What I wanted most for my daughter, however,
was a childhood filled with giggles and the wonderment and joy
of discovering the world and her place in it.

My search for our "right" school didn't stop with preschool.
As a mother, it is my responsibility to examine each school—elementary, middle, high school, and even college—with a critical
eye and the undaunted commitment to find the best learning
opportunities for my children. It is not the right of parents to
serve as their child's advocate, it is their responsibility.

Over the years I have discovered that parenting is a very personal journey. Each child comes into the world a fully unique
being. Whereas I've hoped to foster authenticity, intellect, com-
passion, and intrinsic curiosity in my daughters, other parents
encourage different skills and abilities. Perhaps they want their
child to be the first reader, to master their multiplication facts
by the age of nine, or to accurately recite the periodic chart. As
parents, we differ in our values, in our belief systems, and in our
dreams for our children.

Choice isn't an educational concept; it's basic to the American culture. Visitors from other countries share disbelief at the
number of choices we have the opportunity to make on a rou-
tine basis. We, as Americans, have grown accustomed to having
choices. We are spoiled by the hundreds of cereal boxes on the
breakfast food aisle; the two hundred cable channels plus "picture in picture"; thousands of restaurant choices; millions of
shopping choices; and if we end up with something we don't
like, we can change that too (even our own bodies). Likewise,
our public education system is forced to adapt to the American
culture of free choice.

Four Models of Instruction

While our schools have been adapting to the aspect of parental
choice, they've also had to adapt to political mandates and gov-

ernment reforms that simultaneously undermine choice and institute a "one-size-fits-all" education. Parents and students should have choices beyond selecting a district when moving and which school to attend. The role of schools and teachers is to educate parents about what those choices represent and where they can be found. Fortunately, transitions in education over the past century have provided multiple options. Waldorf, Montessori, Core Knowledge, and experiential learning schools offer a variety of educational models.

Classroom instruction models represent a range of philosophies and techniques. Teachers have their very own experiences, interests, and talents. Some teachers are masterful at lecture and storytelling; others are experts at creating engaging experiences for their students. Standards-based education and high-stakes testing, the primary characteristics of today's reform movement, have generated their own model of instruction and with it significant changes to American classrooms.

For simplicity, I have organized the education styles into four groups: cognitive, constructivist, standards-based, and autonomous. Throughout the history of American public education, these models have changed places in terms of predominance.

The most skillful teachers exercise an array of strategies attempting to meet all students' needs (cognitive, social, and emotional). It's important to understand that these models are not fixed. It is possible for a teacher to utilize various aspects of all of these models during a single lesson.

Understanding these four models is important to recognizing the impact of standardization reforms with regard to our children's academic preparation.

The examples are developed for a fourth-grade classroom and are based on the Anasazi Indians. For comparative purposes I've based each model on the same lesson objective: *Understanding artifacts—how they are discovered and dated and what they tell us about ancient civilization.* The following curriculum topics may also be addressed throughout the various models:

- Location and landscape
- Art and culture
- Anthropology
- Customs and religion

- Shelter and housing
- Archeology and artifacts
- Tools and technology
- Natural resources: farming and hunting
- Political structure and relations
- Development and transitional phases of ancient civilizations

Cognitive Instruction

Cognitive theory was introduced by Jean Piaget. From an educational standpoint, cognitive instruction is based on the assumption that the individual learner is mentally collecting information in order to make sense of knowledge and experience. The learner in this theory relies on his or her mental abilities in order to process information and construct new meaning. Those processes can include problem solving, analyzing, comparing and contrasting, making inferences, scaffolding, and theorizing.

In this cognitive instruction example, students are asked to begin by drawing a picture or writing a story of what they know about dating artifacts and anything related to *stratification, dendrochronology,* and *radio carbon dating.* This exercise engages neurological synapses and gives the teacher information about each student's current level of knowledge.

Then, based on the book *The Village of Blue Stone,* by Stephen Trimble, the teacher tells a narrative about Old Badger Claw. Badger Claw is a fictional character who lived nine centuries ago in the Anasazi tribe as their sun watcher.

The instructor circulates pictures of actual artifacts, or in some cases real artifacts. Students are grouped together to discuss a possible classification system for various artifacts and the method that archeologists would likely use to date them. The teacher introduces the classification system: lithic, bone, ceramic, and vegetal.

After observing the students and posing questions, the teacher assesses their understanding by asking them to consider the Anasazi Indians and write a three-paragraph essay about what artifacts would likely be found in and around the cliff dwellings, their classification, and what the artifacts were likely used for.

The effectiveness of this type of lesson depends on clear and engaging communication and stories that are both memorable and filled with rich details that construct a vivid picture of ancient civilization.

Constructivist—Hands-on Instruction

The second example is constructivist theory. Among its early promoters were John Dewey and Lev Vygotsky, who viewed learning as an active process. Here the student learns through experience. Problem-based learning and discovery learning are two examples of constructivist theory.

This example of instruction begins with students making verbal predictions about artifacts likely to be uncovered near the shelters of Cliff Palace, a well-known ancient Anasazi dwelling. As the students say or write their predictions, the teacher lists them on the chalkboard. Students are then directed to read a section from a *National Geographic Kids* magazine on stratification, dendrochronology, and radiocarbon dating ancient artifacts.

The teacher provides ten to fifteen minutes of direct instruction on archeological procedures and tools and the classification system used to categorize artifacts. Working in groups, students then simulate an archeological dig by graphing off and sifting a teaspoon of sand at a time to uncover "artifacts" (pottery shards, bones, arrow heads, etc.) buried in the playground sandbox. Students collect the "artifacts" and label them according to lithic, bone, ceramic, and vegetal and are also invited to create their own classification system.

Groups present their findings, explaining the challenges they experienced locating and uncovering artifacts and the methodology behind labeling and categorizing their findings. The teacher assesses children's understanding through observations and questioning.

The lesson concludes with a democratic dialogue on what archeologists would likely discover in our trash heaps nine centuries in the future and what those artifacts would lead them to believe about our culture. Lessons like this can leave lasting impressions with children because students are actively engaged through multiple sensory levels, and the learning is personalized and therefore meaningful.

Standards-Based Instruction

The standards-based example begins with the introduction of the standard—History Standard #1a: The student demonstrates an understanding of the chronological organization of historical events and major areas—and Benchmark #3: Knows the chronological order of important events in the creation and the development of the state of Colorado.[1]

The lesson begins with a vocabulary review of terms: *stratification, dendrochronology, radio carbon dating, lithic, bone, ceramic,* and *vegetal.* The teacher passes out the worksheets and reviews the instructions. Students match the pictures of artifacts to the correct word classification by drawing lines. There are a series of multiple-choice or true/false questions about which artifacts would likely be found near cliff dwellings. Students then choose the letter that best matches the answer to the question. For example: "The age of a wooden beam is best determined by (a) stratification; (b) dendrochronology, (c) radiocarbon dating. Children are assessed based on their answers to the questions provided.

Assessments in the standardization model drive instruction and often *become* the instruction. Student activities reflect the structure and form of standardized tests because it is understood that the more exposure to a testing format, the better students will do on the tests. Parents should not be surprised to find that their student's textbooks are issued by the same publishers of the state's tests or by the corporation's subsidiary. For example, Wright Group, publishers of Everyday Math, is owned by McGraw-Hill. As such, standardization ensures that the instruction and curriculum our children are presented each day is entirely driven by a single test.[2]

Singular dimension instruction, which holds children accountable only for lines and letters, reinforces the lowest levels of thinking. The dullness and monotony created by the standards model have a numbing effect both intellectually and emotionally. Students, who are not engaged in the learning process, whether through their interest with the instructor or their excitement over the material, will not assimilate new information. Jan Fortune-Wood makes the case that "irrelevant teaching, or instruction, is more likely to damage than enhance thinking."[3]

Teachers relying on test-level type of questioning have little (if any) insight into a child's real understanding or true ability.

The standards model also requires the least amount of preparation and knowledge from the teacher. Worksheets are the instruction, while standards-based testing covers more concepts; none of the material is addressed with the depth needed for long-term retention.

Colleges and universities are just now beginning to see the effects of children educated under a standardized model. Whatever information students learn is not retained because it is fragmented and disassociated. Students become outsiders to their own learning. They lose the ability to ask their own questions, let alone find their own answers.

Autonomous Instruction

There is yet a fourth example currently making significant headway in alternative schools and homeschooling—autonomous learning. Autonomous learning, also referred to as natural or holistic learning, is difficult to define because autonomous learning takes into consideration a child's interests, learning style, and educational goals.

In accordance with autonomous learning, a study of ancient artifacts and Anasazi Indians would be completely unique for each individual. Some examples may include the making of a short documentary, a trip to the museum, the creation of authentic-looking artifacts, or writing a nonfictional essay or a fictional narrative.

There is a large movement in favor of this approach to learning as well as a large movement opposed to autonomous learning. John Taylor Gatto, New York teacher of the year and author of the book *The Underground History of American Education*, contends, "Kids educated at home are brighter and more impressively human than institutionalized kids, simply because they are allowed to learn free of bells, bogus experts, phony sequences, endless interventions and similar junk."[4]

Speaking personally, it is my experience that natural learning is the most evolved educational approach to human development. However, this level of educational flexibility and respect for both student and teacher does not currently exist in today's public education system, nor can autonomy be mandated or enforced. The level of empowerment necessitated by natural learning is uncomfortable for a great number of people, including teachers and parents.

Having said that, the beauty of autonomous learning is that it will happen, despite artificially established performance skills, mock instruction, or legislated measurement devices. My younger daughter, Sophie, announced at the dinner table that she "had figured a way to daydream while looking directly at the teacher as if she were listening to every word."

Roland Meighan in a column in *Natural Parenting* wrote:

> Parents soon find out that young children are natural learners. They are like explorers or research scientists busily gathering information and making meaning out of the world. Most of this learning is not the result of teaching, but rather a constant and universal learning activity as natural as breathing. Our brains are programmed to learn unless discouraged. A healthy brain stimulates itself by interacting with what it finds interesting or challenging in the world around it. It learns from any mistakes and operates a self-correcting process.[5]

This past summer I asked both my daughters what they would like to learn over their break. My daughter Grace, eleven years old and not having shown much interest in school, decided on cooking, knitting, sewing, singing, and the butterfly swimming stroke. She experienced all of it, except for singing lessons. Now that school is back in session, Grace cooks one night a week for our family and has started compiling a kids' cookbook.

When I asked Sophie, who really loves school, what she would like to learn over the summer, she answered, "I want to sleep in and play outside." So she did, and that too is autonomous learning.

Critics will find fault in this. They will say, "See, if left to their own devices children will not achieve anything." My husband and I believe that a beautiful childhood is appropriate preparation for adulthood and the challenges offered in a real world.

Some years I've made special arrangements with their teachers so that our daughters do not bring school work home or complete "homework." Instead we have long discussions at the dinner table, read, play games, go on walks, write in our journals, and learn through various life experiences.

I must also add, however, that we would never homeschool our children. Though I am disgusted by the direction that public education has taken, I feel strongly that my daughters learn to understand various systems—how to utilize them and when to disregard them. Autonomous learning is not only a recognition of one's own interests, questions, concerns, and problems, but also an awareness of those around them and their process and ideological perspectives. I invite all of the parents who are quite justified in homeschooling to come back to public education and fight for meaningful, challenging, and personalized learning opportunities for all children—even the ones who don't belong to us.

Although these four models of instruction have been simplified for purposes of illustration, they indicate the vast range of theories in learning and instruction. There are many choices to be made by administrators, teachers, parents, and students regarding school governance, curriculum, instructional strategies, assessments, and so forth. If standards-based education were, like Core Knowledge, just another model in the vast array of school options, standardization and high-stakes testing wouldn't be nearly as destructive.

The real crisis in education is that standardized education is forcing out alternative options in today's public schools. A teacher's ability to personalize instruction for his or her students and modify the curriculum is prohibited. Failure to conform to the tests or to raise scores results in heavy sanctions for teachers and students. Parents have no alternatives to the lock-step learning and testing treadmill.

The modern reforms—performance standards and high-stakes testing—have contaminated our classrooms, paralyzed educators, and constrained educational choice in our public school system. Most significant and tragic, today's educational policies are numbing imagination, stifling creativity, and (sometimes literally) putting our future to sleep. Boredom has become the lesson of the day.

Charter School Debate

The introduction of charter schools is integral to the debate over school choice. A charter school is funded with public dollars but is organized and managed outside the district. What's made charter schools so trendy is not their raging success but rather the element of choice. Charter schools have a definite advantage over traditional schools because the families who "choose" to attend have an automatic "buy-in."

An informed and engaged community is one of the primary indicators of a successful school. Many charter schools require parent involvement for enrollment. This process attracts families who value education and seek active participation in the educational process. Many charter schools are also entitled to pick and choose their students, a privilege denied to neighborhood schools.

Still, this hasn't guaranteed success for the charter school model. A 2006 report by the National Center for Education Statistics revealed that fourth-graders attending traditional public schools were significantly better in reading and math than comparable students attending charter schools. Of course, the study's conclusion was based on a sample of 376,000 students' scores on the National Assessment of Education Progress (NAEP). Again, standardized, one-size-fits-all testing was the only measurement.

Because charter schools are a fairly recent phenomenon, little additional research has been done examining their effectiveness. A couple of independent studies looking at longitudinal growth and achievement beyond graduation have emerged, but they were limited to individual schools. Factors that affect the quality of a charter school are the same as those affecting public schools: common focus, strong leadership, qualified and empowered teachers, involved community, engaged students, and the like. The bottom line is that there are some examples of exceptional charter schools, just as there are examples of exceptional public schools.

Other than choice, the value of charter schools (and magnet schools as well) is differentiation. Schools are more often a reflection of the community they serve. School districts with the flexibility and authority to be responsive to the specific needs and values of unique students and communities are far more effective. The benefit of the charter school movement is that it has spurred greater diversity in our educational system. Public schools that voluntarily diversify their school's models, philosophies, programs, and courses will ultimately have an advantage over districts that remain uniform.

The criticism of charter schools is that they create a two-tiered system with special rights and privileges afforded only to charter school students. Inequities in expectations and regulations inherent to the charter school movement must be addressed and rectified. For example, some charter schools require parents to raise a specified amount of money or volunteer for a certain number of hours. Charter schools also pull scarce funds and resources away from neighborhood schools, something traditional private and parochial schools have never done.

Although the vast majority of Americans report a high degree of satisfaction with their neighborhood schools,[6] the climate of budget cuts, expensive bureaucracy, declining enrollments, and the expansion of charter schools have contributed to the closing of neighborhood schools. As more and more schools shut their doors, the cannibalizing impact of charter schools is sure to be felt.

While proponents celebrate the expansion of charter schools, thousands of children find themselves bidding tearful good-byes to their neighborhood schools. Parents are just now beginning to recognize the unintended consequence of charter schools as they fight to keep their neighborhood schools open. We must take care that one parent's choice does not come at the expense of another's.

The Magic of Magnet Schools

Advances in brain research and scientific developments have shed more light on how human beings learn. Now more than ever before, teachers have empirical evidence reinforcing the concept that children learn differently. This new understanding over the decades has led to an awareness of the need to differentiate and modify instruction, as well as theories and models like multiple intelligence, content integration and immersion (i.e., theme planning), experiential learning, authentic assessment, and magnet schools.

Magnet schools are often confused with charter schools. The difference is that magnet schools are organized and managed from within the district. They are similar to charter schools because they are structured around a specific educational philosophy, such as the arts, science and technology, bilingual education, British Primary, International Baccalaureate, or Montessori, to name a few. Unlike charter schools, magnet schools do not bleed scarce resources from the district school budget.

The purpose behind magnet schools is to cultivate the individual abilities of each child and to promote racial and socioeconomic integration. Student demographics for charter schools, in contrast, are much more homogenous.

Interestingly, the magnet school model was expanding at the same time the *Nation at Risk* report was claiming that neighborhood schools were failing. Public school leaders had become aware that the "one-size-fits-all" model was no longer appropriate to the needs of America's burgeoning diverse student population and global challenges.

Changes associated with learning acquisition, brain development, and the public's demand for more options led to the expansion of magnet schools. In the early 1980s, magnet schools began to emerge in districts throughout the nation. The book *Definitive Studies of Magnet Schools: Voices of Public School Choice*[7] highlights some of the most successful magnet schools and the research related to their student learning and achievement.

The Jeffco Open School in Lakewood, Colorado, offers instruction from preschool through twelfth grade and for the past thirty-five years has provided a "viable, vibrant, and life-changing alternative to conventional schooling." A recent longitudinal survey indicated that a robust 95 percent of the school's graduates who were surveyed reported "that the Jeffco Open School had a positive influence on their lives."[8]

The problem is that at the same time magnet schools were promoting differentiation and personalization, the nation was adopting a model instituting uniformity and conformity. In 1993, as the Magnet School Assistance Program began disbursing funds, President Bill Clinton was drafting Goals 2000, requiring every state to adopt statewide standards by 2000.

The later mandates of the No Child Left Behind Act established a single definition of school quality: high test scores. Noncompliant schools—including magnets, charters, alternative, and innovative schools—are penalized. The knowledge of teachers and authority of parents has been usurped by federal and state controls reinforcing rote learning, linear thinking, and the standard of mediocrity.

The few remaining magnet schools are constantly negotiating the challenges of having to conform to minimal competency requirements while infusing innovation and individualism into their classrooms.

Education critics and politicians have forwarded a conflicting message—a demand for school choice together with a demand for uniform achievement. If schools are to invite innovation and provide alternative forms of teaching and learning, we will have to revise the current notion of learning and achievement.

Magnet schools can provide the answer to cultivating the talents of our youth and diversifying public education. However, government representatives will first have to remove the barriers to school leadership, teacher expertise, student empowerment, and parent involvement. Rather than conformity and uniformity we need government leaders to value ingenuity and differentiation, which means getting government out of the daily operations of education.

The Story of Cole: A Case Study

In 1994 I completed my student teaching at McKinley Thatcher Elementary School in Denver, Colorado. My students were fifth graders, continuing on to one of three middle schools. The most popular choice at that time was Cole, which turned away half its applicants. Cole was a thriving School of the Arts magnet program and included a diverse socioeconomic and racial student population.

Due to severe budget constraints, Denver Public Schools in 1997 ended its school busing program and terminated twenty-three years of desegregation efforts. Students who were deemed as living too far away from the school they attended were promptly sent bus passes for the city's public transportation, RTD. That same year, the School of the Arts program was moved and Cole was transformed back into a traditional middle school serving some of Denver's poorest neighborhoods.

In 2000, Colorado passed Senate Bill 186, a stricter version of the No Child Left Behind Act. Under this legislation, schools were graded according to a single indicator—test scores. According to the initial law, schools scoring "low" were to be closed and reconstituted as charter schools.

Despite after-school and weekend test preparation seminars, in which even Denver's mayor, John Hickenlooper, volunteered, Cole's scores on standardized tests remained low. Cole was closed in 2005. Ironically, the state could find no interested chartering authority willing to assume responsibility for the academic achievement of poor minority children.

Finally, the Knowledge Is Power Program (KIPP), arrived from California with some stringent demands. With fifty-two schools in sixteen states, KIPP boasts a vision to "put underserved students on the path to college." KIPP was not successful at putting Cole's students on the path to college, nor was it able to put them on the path to high school. KIPP served grades seven and eight in the 2005–2006 school year, grade eight in 2006–2007, and then shut its doors. Reasons for the failure are unclear or not clearly stated.

Ten years will have passed since the School of the Arts program was removed from Cole. Ten years have been squandered and hundreds of children transitioned or abandoned. Government mandates and poor policy decisions undermined educational innovation and an effective school. Cole is just one example in a string of hundreds where children have paid—and continue to pay—the price of misguided education reforms.

Vouchers and Gougers

In today's highly polarized political climate, there is no greater consensus builder than the cause of children. The debate over vouchers, however, draws clear political lines. Proponents of vouchers build their argument on the values of free enterprise and market-like competition. They claim that competition is the key to educational improvement and that whatever government can do, private enterprise can do better.

What proponents of vouchers continue to overlook is that America is not just an economy. This country is defined by its unique political structure, a social structure strengthened by diverse cultural and religious freedom, and a free-market economic structure. To reconstitute our educational system on economic principles alone is oversimplistic and counterproductive.

The theory behind vouchers also directly conflicts with basic economic principles. If vouchers were to be instituted, the demand for private schools would likely increase. When demand goes up, price goes up—in this case, our taxes. The deregulation and privatization of energy, for example, has led to higher prices for the consumer. Yet, the same people arguing for vouchers continue to argue for tax cuts. What they conveniently overlook is that keeping pace with commercial market demands and toe-stepping to the profit-centered ideal will eventually require higher taxes.

Economically disadvantaged children still can't afford private tuition, uniforms, transportation, or the additional fees associated with private schools. The American people continue to say "no" to vouchers because they aren't interested in subsidizing affluent families and private schools. Despite the enormous financing behind pro-voucher campaigns, voters in Michigan, California, Colorado, and most recently Utah and Arizona have killed ballot initiatives that create statewide voucher policies.

Private campaign financers and conservative foundations (mostly in outside states) spend millions during election years, supporting pro-voucher candidates and ballot initiatives. One of their most notable claims is that "vouchers are a valuable tool for helping needy children escape failing public schools." Not true. Vouchers transfer the limited dollars away from our educational infrastructure. Low-income families don't want an escape; they want strong local schools, safe neighborhoods, and involved communities. The correct answer is to fund schools in poor neighborhoods, promoting academic success for the neediest children.

Modified voucher programs in Cleveland, Milwaukee, and Florida have created a two-tiered system where private schools operate with a different set of regulations and accountability tools than public schools. Directing public dollars to organizations not responsible to the public is counter to the ongoing demand for greater transparency and school accountability.

It's interesting to note that the reformers making the case for vouchers are often the same individuals advocating for more restrictive regulation and greater state and federal control of public schools, which exempts the private schools they are promoting. On one hand, they support bills like NCLB, which expanded bureaucracy and federal regulations; on the other, they campaign to turn our children and our tax dollars over to schools that will have neither. This ideological inconsistency should lead the public to question the motives behind various reform initiatives and slogans such as "no child left behind."

Vouchers also promote economic and racial segregation. "Separate but equal" was the ideology leading to legalized discrimination against African Americans and Asians in theaters, restrooms, buses, restaurants, hotels, churches, schools, and in-numerable other situations. Have we not already learned this lesson? Separate is not equal. Ever.

The matter of church and state is also integral to the vouchers debate. Many Americans support both the institutions of religion and government. The United States is among the most religiously diverse countries in the world, thanks in part to the First Amendment to the United States Constitution and the highly contested constitutional provision for separation between church and state.

With regard to vouchers and the use of public tax dollars for private schooling, it's important to remember that approximately 85 percent of private schools in this country are religious. To uphold the second clause of the First Amendment—ensuring freedom regarding the practice and expression of faith—government must not take sides.[9] Nor can Congress make "laws respecting an establishment of religion." U.S. tax dollars therefore should never go to institutions that discriminate or deliver services based on religion. Respect for religious differences is basic to American and democratic principles.

Because it is based on a concept that undermines the foundations of public education, the voucher movement has made only small gains throughout the decades. Our forefathers recognized that an educated citizenry was essential to a successful democracy, a prosperous economy, and the advancement of society. Abraham Lincoln in his first political speech gave us these words: "Upon the subject of education, not presuming to dictate any plan or system respecting it, I can only say that I view it as the most important subject which we as a people can be engaged in."[10]

Private schools have existed for centuries now. Although there are some exceptional examples, private education has not proved its superiority to public education. Enrollment in private education has remained relatively flat over the past quarter-century. Since standardization and the 1994 announcement of Goals 2000, we have seen only a 1 percent increase in private school enrollment.[11]

We are a nation that although frustrated and concerned, supports public education. Much like our transportation system with its roads, bridges, railroads, and ports that sustain trade, commerce, the delivery of goods, travel, and basic commuting, public education is a necessary infrastructure. Our entire nation would come to an absolute halt without a transportation system, and our nation will equally collapse if we do not sustain and work collectively to improve, and not dismantle, our educational infrastructure.

Failed Priorities

Another huge misconception in the education debate suggests that defenders of democracy are at odds with defenders of capitalism. Not so. The values of democracy have been aligned with the values of a free market since the inception of this country. The conflict rests with the enterprise system itself. Corporations who put cost-cutting before development continue to pay the price associated with greed.

The American auto industry, for example, subjugated its advantage by being slower at developing new technology, especially in the area of efficiency. The industry has been undermined by its own focus on reducing costs rather than investing in new technologies, quality designs, and fuel-efficient automobiles.

The fate of public education may simply come down to America being too cheap to advance its most valuable resources: our people. The capitalist mantra "best product for the lowest price" may apply to cars, but it is an oxymoron in education. The bottom line in consumer terms is "you get what you pay for." We are simply not going to produce the most highly skilled, well-educated, and developed citizenry on the cheap. Clyde Prestowitz, author of *Three Billion New Capitalists: The Great Shift of Power to the East*, reports that the United States will fail in a global economy if we do not begin making the necessary investments in infrastructure, research and development, and education.[12]

Education critics often claim that spending more money hasn't improved education. That's a true statement, but only because the money has been spent on the wrong things—standardized tests, bureaucratic procedures, and flashy reports. Money does make a difference if spent wisely! Smaller class sizes, safe school buildings, computers, electronics, and after-school programs make a difference, not for politicians, but for kids.[13]

Goodwin Liu, assistant professor of law at the University of California–Berkeley, explains the correlation between higher achievement as measured by the NAEP and educational spending:

> Student performance varies considerably from state to state. While 35% of fourth-graders nationwide achieved proficiency on the NAEP math test in 2005, state figures ranged from 49% in Massachusetts to 19% in Mississippi and New Mexico. The states below the national average are almost all low-spending states in the South, Southwest, and Far West.[14]

An undeniable case can be made that greater investments in education have in fact yielded greater student achievement. The converse is also true for those students who are denied the resources and the opportunities.

Making the Right Choices

American parents have educational choice. They can choose homeschooling, neighborhood schools, or, for many Americans, private schools. In fact, many states offer open enrollment between schools and districts. Provided they can afford it, families have the option of moving to any one of the nearly 16,000 school districts throughout the United States. That's choice.

The continued debate over choice doesn't have to be an either/or proposition. Improving our schools involves diversifying and expanding educational choices for parents, students, and teachers.

We must also work to make children and public education a national priority. It is not just a matter of *having* choices but also a matter of *making* the right choices. We have committed ourselves to having the greatest national defense in the world, and we have succeeded. We have not committed ourselves to having the greatest educational system in the world.

6

Solutions

One morning in my first year of teaching, I took attendance, registered the lunch count, and began to go over the day's schedule—division, ecosystems, identifying important details in our reading, and so forth. I looked out at the young faces and then asked my students this question: "What would you like to learn today?" Their heads poked up and their eyes grew wide as they looked around, confused. I said, "You don't think I come to school every day for *my* benefit, do you?" Their eyes got wider. "The purpose of your education is you," I continued:

> The goal is not what you learn today; the goal is to expand your capacity to learn every day. Division and ecosystems are not going to carry you through your life. What will is the ability to learn from your experience—whatever the experience. You're not here to master facts and meaningless details, you're here to develop the patterns, the behaviors, and the curiosity to answer life's most important questions: who are you, what will you know, and how will "what you've learned" and "who you have become" contribute to the larger world?

My students responded with a volley of questions both practical and philosophical.[1]

In their book *Freakonomics*, Steven Levitt and Stephen Dubner examine what makes a perfect parent.[2] Using the Early Childhood Longitudinal Study (ECLS) conducted by the U.S. Department of Education with 20,000 children from kindergarten through fifth grade, Levitt and Dubner considered a vast number of variables correlating to children's "standardized test scores" (of course!). The study asked the question, "What kind of parenting is associated with a child's achievement?" The data leads to some interesting, but not surprising, revelations.

For example, a child who has "many books in the home" is correlated with higher test scores, but the fact that a child's "parents read to them every day" does not. A child with a parent "involved in the PTA" is a correlating factor, but "the child frequently watches television" is not. Subjecting all of the data to regression analysis, the two economists ultimately concluded that the list of indicators correlating to student achievement described things that parents "are" and not the things that parents "do." Their analysis offers insights far beyond the topic of education. The data points to the one conclusion we've known all along but keep forgetting—it's the people that make the difference.

What is most important in our schools, in our homes, in our businesses, and in our communities is not the numbers or the data, but "who we are."

When we become a nation of citizens, of intellectuals, of substance, of conviction, then who we "are" will inform what we "do." Only then can we can begin to:

- Design and invest in a first-rate public education system
- End childhood poverty
- Ensure that every child has health care
- Protect children and public safety in every community
- Nurture abandoned, neglected, and abused children as if they were our own
- Reduce incarcerations and prison inmates
- Minimize drug and alcohol addiction
- Decrease teen pregnancies
- Stop children from killing themselves and each other

I have had the privilege of looking at education through the eyes of each of the stakeholders: student, teacher, parent, administrator, and policymaker. I have spent a large part of my life sorting through the rhetoric, propaganda, case studies, and the research. I have examined "who's to blame" and "how to fix it." The purpose of this book is to help you, the deciding public, understand today's educational policies and the long-term consequences of current education reforms.

What exists now is the opportunity to create a different experience for each of us—children, educators, administrators, parents, legislators, and citizens. At this point I would like to invite you to join in creating a new vision so that together we may begin to improve the lives of children and transform public education and our future.

A Teacher's Note

I begin with you, teachers, because you are the heart of education. If you feel that you have been unfairly blamed or ridiculed, you are justified in your feelings. I won't attempt to excuse the frequent condemnations, but I will offer this explanation: *The whole world recognizes the significance and the influence of teachers.*

Your silence and neutrality have not served the children. Policy abuses and budget neglect have gone too far in part because you have allowed it. It is time that you speak loudly and carry a big stick. Our children are what are at stake here, and we've already compromised too much in the way of our profession and values.

Think about what you need to do your best job: safe climates, supportive leaders, time to work, space to rest, opportunities to play, inspiration to excel, resources, tools, a nurturing social network, fresh air for breathing. . . . It really is a simple formula. My advice to you is to create this for yourselves and then create it for your students.

It's our job as adults to model, lead, encourage, and inspire. The job of our children is to make mistakes. That is the very way they grow up and become adults who can model, lead, encourage, and inspire. We've accepted this model of treating children like gadgets on an assembly line because we misinterpret mistakes to mean failure. *Mistakes are not failure*—mistakes are very important opportunities for learning. Classrooms need not only cultivate right answers but also provide an environment in which mistakes are plentiful and so is the learning.

There are countless examples all over this country of exceptional teachers making an extraordinary difference every day. Examples include schools that have created partnerships with local growers to deliver healthy, fresh, and nutritious meals to students. Many businesses have joined efforts with community schools to provide after-school tutoring, apprenticeships, mentoring, chess clubs, and kick ball. Thank you to the Mrs. Williams who teach Newton's Law of Gravity by having students carry a rock up hill. Appreciation goes to the secretaries who teach children how to smile and the janitors who offer a weekly joke. Recognition for the Mr. Hills who give kids a reason to climb the classroom steps just because they can feel the love. We pay tribute to the Ms. LaGuardias who inspire students to write with pictures of art, newspaper articles, and famous speeches. Bravo, bravo, bravo to you all.

In this climate of standardization and high-stakes testing, never forget that your two primary objectives are to engage your learners and cultivate something extraordinary in each child.

A Meeting with the Principal

School administrators know very well that the purpose of our educational system from its inception has been to develop the American citizenry. George Washington in his Farewell Address of 1796 said, "Promote then, as an object of importance, institutions for the general diffusion of knowledge. In proportion as the structure of government gives force to public opinion, it is essential that public opinion should be enlightened."

Research in cognitive theory, trends in constructivism, social movements, metaphysics, and even pop culture have proposed a second purpose for public schooling: development of the individual. The Industrial Revolution and the "efficiency movement" introduced a third purpose—to prepare students—not as citizens, but as workers. Rather than remain locked in battle, it's time we move forward and make way for a multipurpose educational approach.

At a recent community forum on education, one of the councils identified ten goals for students in education, including the following:

- Workforce equipped for the twenty-first century
- Global understanding
- Responsible citizens, world contributors
- Critical thinkers and problem solvers
- Education for the whole child (intellectual, emotional, physical, subjective)

Similar collaborations are taking place across the country in which the dialogue seeks a broader and deeper understanding of the educational process and more meaningful goals for our future leaders. Although these are the kinds of goals we should be working toward, so long as we have a single indicator of student achievement and school quality (test scores), our classrooms will never reflect these values, and neither will our children.

So what are the indicators of a powerful citizenry, the finest workforce, and developed human beings? Lawmakers will no doubt be looking for quantifiable measurements. I'd suggest that we start with the obvious. You'll know our schools are improving when a greater number of young adults are making their way to vocational training and college and fewer are making their way to jail. You'll know we're successful when more students are graduating from high school and fewer are graduating from rehabilitation centers.

Additional quantifiable indicators may include:

- full voter participation
- higher employment rates
- significant drops in incarcerations
- lower rates of recidivism
- fewer youth suicides and attempts
- declining acts of abuse and neglect
- reduction in homelessness
- a decrease in drug and alcohol incidents and addictions
- increased community involvement in public schools
- a greater percentage of high school graduates
- more college and secondary school graduates
- overall economic gains and a growing economy
- an influx of teachers into the education profession
- an increased rate of teacher retention

These are only some of the measures that begin to reflect our social, political, and economic values.

Lobbyists today play an important role in shaping public policy. I feel very strongly that the best education lobbyists are those who have taught in the classroom themselves. Still, they cannot take the place of 1,000 teachers or 20,000 parents. Educational leaders, not lobbyists, have got to do a better job of educating the policymakers.

I have witnessed the powerful impact of a superintendent's testimony during legislative hearings. School districts that bring teachers and parents to the capitol to speak with legislators and testify are influential in the policy arena and are more effective in representing children's interests. Lobbyists must always be carefully scrutinized. Every district needs to formally publish its school boards, teachers, administrators, parents, and representing lobbyists' policy positions (both active and passive) regarding all state legislation and local policies. It's time to demand that all of the stakeholders and power players come out of the dark.

Legislators should also be invited into the schools. High schools are the perfect setting for candidate debates on budget priorities and financing our schools. Political dialogue and exposure to candidates also help to engage students in the democratic process.

It is up to you, superintendents, principals, and deans, to begin to change the conversations and move our classrooms toward meaningful, challenging, and personalized learning. Teachers often say to me, "Our meetings used to be about children; now all we talk about are test scores." School leaders set the tone. Let's begin to discuss a new vision for our schools and our children in our faculty meetings, PTOs, back-to-school-nights, staff development seminars, and parent-teacher conferences. Then expand those conversations into our Chamber of Commerce buildings, city halls, and state capitols. Educators are the experts, and they should be leading the discussions about how to improve our public schools.

Changing the conversation, however, is only the beginning. Together let us champion the Marva Collinses of the world who used Shakespeare and the classics to teach her students to read and to lead.[3] It's time to listen to the Deborah Meierses who opened schools in communities and worked with parents, teachers, students, and local citizens to build a community in a school.[4] There are also those less famous, like the rural Colorado superintendent Gerald Keefe, who took a salary cut before cutting teachers' salaries and was the first school administrator to say "no" to the No Child Left Behind Act. Or the Denver superintendent who moved his administrative offices into a community school to save money, improve teacher/administrator relations, and avoid yet another school closure.

There are those too who have given us a whole new model of education, like Sudbury, Cristo Rey, MET, and Essential Schools.[5] Schools have partnered with senior services, mental health departments, judicial departments, and developmental disability organizations to share resources, expand children's support systems, and facilitate new ideas. The Queens Library in New York has transformed itself into a full-service learning center for kids, teens, adults, and seniors. The Chicago Board of Education has partnered with both the Chicago Recreation District and Library District to develop the Sports 37 teen initiative offering after-school programs and activities at eighteen schools.

Mapleton Public Schools in Denver, Colorado, was the first district in the country to begin the long and gradual process of differentiating each of its schools. The "reinvention campaign" has meant restructuring traditional schools into specialized schools, including Montessori, arts, technology, and leadership.[6] In terms of test scores, initial results have been mixed. In terms of strengthening communities and addressing the diverse needs of students, success is growing. Differentiation may at first appear a complicated proposition. The process of implementing different school models, such as magnet schools, and then accepting heterogeneous definitions of quality will indeed ensure variations between schools—as it should. That's life. If our goal is to prepare children for life, then life is what the classroom experience should reflect. We have done a great disservice to children in our commitment to create a uniform learning environment—the world is not uniform, and neither are they.

Those in power will have to resist the tendency to dictate common solutions. Innovation requires resources and conditions that promote trust and experimentation. Too often, efforts to control the uncertainties compromise imagination and collaboration—two essentials for extraordinary schools and classrooms.

A Call Home to All Moms, Dads, and Caregivers

This year, as always during the period of high-stakes testing, my daughters and I will visit museums, walk the dogs at the animal shelter, paint outdoor scenery, and read books. I do not ask the school for permission to opt out of the federally mandated tests. I do not seek consent from my government representatives for my children to be absent on those days. These are my children, and their education is my responsibility.

As parents, my husband and I will not allow our children to be used as monitors for the state nor will we allow their learning to be reduced to shaded ovals. We support our schools and we support our teachers. We deliver our children to their doorsteps every morning because we trust them. We want our daughter's teacher, along with our input and hers, to determine her educational decisions—not the mayor, not the governor, and not even the president!

Parents' and teachers' refusal to comply with high-stakes testing is not an act of defiance, but an act of courage. As Dr. Martin Luther King Jr. explained, "Nonviolent direct action seeks to create such a crisis and foster such a tension that a community which has constantly refused to negotiate is forced to confront the issue." In his letter from a Birmingham, Alabama, jail cell, he goes on to write,

> I am cognizant of the interrelatedness of all communities and states. I cannot sit idly by in Atlanta and not be concerned about what happens in Birmingham. Injustice anywhere is a threat to justice everywhere. We are caught in an inescapable network of mutuality, tied in a single garment of destiny. Whatever affects one directly, affects all indirectly.

It is my hope that we can begin to honor the principled teachers like Don Perl and Carl Chew, who have taken an ethical and moral stand in their refusal to administer state tests in the same way we honor our heroes of the civil rights movement.[7] If even a small portion of our population will join in this one act of resistance, high-stakes testing would be abolished by the following year. Rosa Parks and the thousands who carpooled and walked for miles during the Birmingham bus boycott showed us how to change the political course.

I live in a community where parent volunteers spend hundreds of hours on fund-raisers. It's time to table the wrapping paper sales and the bake-offs, and start knocking down the doors of Congress.

Determining priorities and allocating federal resources is our business and involves our dollars. America's children can no longer afford for parents, teachers, and citizens to be passive in the political arena. In the words of Thomas Jefferson, "I know no safe depositor of the ultimate powers of society but the people themselves; and if we think them not enlightened enough to exercise their control with wholesome discretion, the remedy is not to take it from them, but to inform their discretion."[8]

Appendix B is a resource guide for organizations and individuals working toward child-centered education solutions. You are requested to join, to give, to volunteer, to speak out, to help. These are our children, and it's up to us to make the changes they deserve and that our future requires.

A Pink Slip for Policymakers

Steven Wolk, professor of the teacher education department at Northeastern Illinois University, states it most clearly: "There is no neutral ground here; we have decisions to make. Either we remake our schools into vibrant workshops for personal, social, and global transformation, or we must own up to our complicity in perpetuating a superficial, unthinking, and unjust world."[9]

I want to be very clear here with today's government representatives and policy leaders: our children's classrooms are not your political playground. We are tired of words. We are ready for action. It's time to talk less and accomplish more.

Government has its function, but the imposition of standardization, high-stakes testing, and the accompanying unnecessary and inconsequential accounting has created barriers to advancing our educational system and attracting and retaining extraordinary educators. State governments should monitor schools through accreditation; regulate teachers through degrees, certifications, licenses, and background checks; and leave the evaluation of students to professional educators, parents, and elected school boards. This is real accountability, and it is more than adequate. School labels and ratings, like the ones created by NCLB, are just politics. They are costly, grossly simplistic, and inaccurate.

Educational reforms over the past two decades have obliterated services and consumed resources previously directed at increasing opportunities for high-risk children and balancing social inequities. As a result, we continue to lose state revenues to costs associated with unemployment, incarceration, and remediation services.

Although program recommendations should not be prescriptive, state and local government leaders must work with districts to remove barriers, identify resources, and develop partnerships that are responsive to the needs of children. If we want our children to thrive, then we must do more than grade their schools. We will have to ensure safe beds for their rest, warm meals for their nourishment, parks or playgrounds for their exploration, and physicians for their care. Parents, teachers, counselors, school nurses, police officers, business leaders, legislators, and citizens who make an unyielding commitment to the total well-being of all children are the answer.

Our educational system and our children have weathered the goals of President Clinton with standardization and accreditation; they have endured the plans of President Bush's high-stakes testing and school ratings; they will even accept the vision of President Obama for a world-class work force and college accessibility. Our teachers and our children are not short on educational goals, plans, and visions. What they are short on are the resources: the people, the dollars, the time to accomplish high standards, proficient test scores, excellent school ratings, and now "college readiness." So please, in your financial and policy estimations, do not deliver another promise that will not carry with it the resources to serve our children and our shared values.

Student Conference

If you are at the point that you are able to read this book, then you can understand that your education belongs to you. The adults—parents, teachers, administrators, policymakers—can do our part. Yet if you don't begin to make the connections between what you know today and who you will become tomorrow, our efforts will be in vain. So much is up to you.

Just as it is important for us to say "yes" to the experiences that build our understanding and support our direction, it is also important for us to say "no" to the exercises that numb our senses, silence our thinking mind, and drown out our inner knowing voice.

As for students—your job is to determine what learning experiences, teachers, schools, classes, resources, and opportunities have value to you. Pursue sparks of interest and moments of curiosity with absolute persistence, because one day you are going to recognize the power of your own education. Eventually you will discover how all of your wisdom and how all of your abilities culminate to serve a unique purpose. Perhaps you will learn too how your unique purpose benefits your family, your community, and the greater world.

There will always be competing agendas, limited resources, and political dissent. We will always be negotiating who to become and what kind of world we want to live in. Our Constitution was created not so that government could shape our political, economic, and social systems but so that we the people could. And we have. Young people throughout history on campuses and street corners have played a pivotal role in the women's suffrage movement, equality and civil rights, improving working conditions for United Farm Workers, and ending the Vietnam War. Democracy cannot be ensured from the comfort of our sofas. It requires action, intelligence, and courage. Independence is not something that is given but rather an experience that is claimed.

Determination, imagination, and people working hard together have made the difference throughout our history. Before us is the opportunity to change our schools into challenging, personalized, and meaningful places for learning in all capacities. For those who ask, "Where do we begin?" the answer is so very simple:

With you.

Have you heard the story of stone soup? There lies a village that is deeply divided, overcome with fear and famine. A stranger comes to the village and is greeted with slammed doors and closed curtains. Using only a large pot and some stones, he makes a fire and begins making soup. The residents remain in hiding at first, but soon they grow curious and leave the security of their dwellings. The stranger invites each one to contribute something. Mothers, proprietors, farmers, grandfathers, and children bring something to add to the pot: cabbage, a piece of meat, carrots, potatoes, spices, and herbs. Before long they have a delicious soup brewing. The villagers—in spite of fear, in the face of deep division—give of themselves and together create something worthwhile and sustaining.

What will you contribute to our children?
What seeds will you plant for our future?

Appendix A:
Alabama High School Lesson Plan

The following is excerpted from the Alabama Department of
Education performance standards adopted in 1999, effective for
the 2001–2002 school year, accessed at http://www.alsde.edu/
html/home.asp.

Standard V: The student will use appropriate organizational
skills for writing/revising.

Objective 1: Determine logical progression and complete-
ness of paragraphs.

Eligible Content:

- Introductory sentences
- Concluding sentences
- Sequence of events or details
- Transitional words
- Irrelevant and/or redundant sentences

AHSGE Number of Questions: 10

Prerequisites: Writing complete sentences with a variety of
sentence patterns

Course of Study References: Grades 10 and 11 Checklists

Lesson/Teaching Strategies

Getting Started

The purpose of this lesson is to assist students in recognizing a
well-written paragraph. The definitions of an introductory sentence and a concluding sentence should be stressed to help stu-

dents write in paragraph form. The importance of sequence of events and details should be presented as a logical means to communicate, and these details can appear in logical order easily if the student is encouraged to use transitional words and expressions. The distraction of irrelevant or redundant sentences should be modeled so that the student can recognize that they are not appropriate.

Activity 1

Procedure

To encourage students to create a well-written paragraph, the teacher may choose one of many "fairy tales" with which the students would be familiar. "Goldilocks and the Three Bears" works well because of the story's pattern of events. Students should be encouraged to take notes as the teacher reads the story from an elementary-level picture book. Students should then brainstorm or cluster the facts about Goldilocks's character and temperament based on her actions during the story's plot. A picture book allows the students to form statements about Goldilocks from the pictures as well as the story itself. After these ideas about Goldilocks have been listed on the board, students form a basic idea about Goldilocks's behavior based on the events of the story. This idea should result in an introductory sentence for a paragraph about Goldilocks. Her behaviors should form details for the body of the paragraph. To end the paragraph, students can be guided to reach a conclusion based on the fact that Goldilocks ran home without apologizing.

Sample Student Paragraph: Ask students to number the sentences of their paragraph. This makes it possible for other students to follow easily the discussion and to visualize the sentences as they are being discussed.

1. Goldilocks was a rude young girl. 2. She entered the bears' home uninvited. 3. Without hesitation she tasted all three bowls of porridge, which were obviously not prepared for her. 4. The chairs looked so inviting that she sat in all three and even broke one chair. 5. After she broke a chair, she grew tired and sampled all three of the bears' beds for comfort. 6. Goldilocks's sister had a brass bed. 7. Because she did not apologize to the

bears, the reader can assume that Goldilocks needs to develop better manners.

Examples

1. Which of the sentences in the above paragraph is the introductory sentence?
    A. 2
    B. 4
    C. 7
    D. 1

2. Which sentence in the above paragraph is unrelated to the main idea in the paragraph? Why?
    A. 2
    B. 6
    C. 3
    D. 4

3. Which is the concluding sentence? Why?
    A. 4
    B. 5
    C. 6
    D. 7

Solutions

1. D
2. B. This sentence is not related to the topic.
3. D. It is not only the last, but it "wraps up" the evidence presented.

Appendix B: Resource Guide

http://www.angelaengel.com
http://www.deborahmeier.com

Children and Public Education Advocates

National

Educator Roundtable, http://www.educatorroundtable.org
Every Child Matters, http://www.everychildmatters.gov.uk
Fair Test, http://www.fairtest.org
Mothers Acting Up, http://www.mothersactingup.org
National Urban League, http://www.nul.org/
National Women's Law Center, http://www.nwlc.org/
Parents United for Public Schools, http://www.parentsunited.
    org/home.html
People for the American Way, http://www.pfaw.org/

Local

Alliance for Childhood, http:///www.allianceforchildhood.org
Citizens United for Responsible Education, http://www.cure
    washington.org/index.shtml

Parents and Educators

http://www.citizenschools.org
http://www.educationonrevolution.org
http://www.educatorroundtable.org
http://www.inspiredteaching.org

http://www.naturallearninginstitute.org
http:/blogs.edweek.org/edweek/Bridging-Differences/

Calling for a National Boycott to High-Stakes Testing

Students Against Testing, http://www.nomoretests.com
California Coalition for Authentic Reform in Education, http://
www.calcare.org/
Coalition for Better Education, http://www.thecbe.org

Research

National Council for Accreditation of Teacher Education

Maintains links for every state education department,
http:///www.ncate.org/resources/statelinks.htm

National Center for Education Statistics

Public school data, http://www.nces.ed.gov

Net Action

Training for Web-based activism, http://netaction.org/training.
Rethinking Schools, online magazine, http://www.rethinking
schools.org/about/index.shtml.
Susan Ohanian chronicles an online database, http://susan
ohanian.org.

Notes

CHAPTER 1: HIGH-STAKES TESTING

1 E. Mavis Hetherington and Ross D. Parke, *Child Psychology: A Contemporary Viewpoint,* 4th ed. (Columbus, OH: McGraw-Hill, 1993), 375–377.

2 D. J. Swiegers and Louw, eds., *Inleiding tot die Psigologie,* 2nd ed. (Johannesburg: McGraw-Hill, 1982), 145.

3 Stephen Jay Gould, *The Mismeasure of Man* (New York: W. W. Norton, 1981), 151–152, cited in Robert Osgood, "Intelligence Testing and the Field of Learning Disabilities: A Historical and Critical Perspective," *Learning Disability Quarterly* 7 (1984): 343–348.

4 Alain F. Corcos and Floyd Monaghan, *Gregor Mendel's Experiments on Plant Hybrids: A Guided Study* (New Brunswick, NJ: Rutgers University Press, 1993).

5 Alan Stoskepf, *The Forgotten History of Eugenics* 13, 3, Rethinking Schools Online (Spring 1999), http://www.rethinkingschools.org/archive/13_03/eugenics.

6 Lewis Terman, *The Measurement of Intelligence*, Teachers Training Manual (1916), 91–92.

7 Horace Mann Bond, "Intelligence Tests and Propaganda" (1924), 64.

8 Sarah Glazer, "Intelligence Testing: Do Traditional IQ Tests Overlook Some Bright Students?" CQ Researcher, July 30, 1993, 660.

9 Hetherington and Parke, *Child Psychology*, 374.

10 Colorado Student Assessment Program released Reading Item Grade 8, Colorado Department of Education, "Sample CSAP Tests for the LPS Community," 6–8, "Egrets" by Judith Wright from *Collected Poems 1942–1970,* copyright © by Judith Wright. Used by permission of Harper Collins Publishers, Australia, and by permission of Atheneum Books for Young Readers, an imprint of Simon & Schuster Children's Publishing Division.

11 Peter Schuler, "Hillocks Finds that Standardized Writing Assessments May Be Harmful to Children's Learning," *Chicago Chronicle* 21, July 11, 2002.

12 Dr. William Spady, personal conversation, May 1, 2008. *Beyond Counterfeit Reforms: Forging an Authentic Future for All Learners* (Lanham, MD: Scarecrow Press, 2001).

13 Gerald Bracey, "The Condition of Public Education," *Phi Delta Kappan*, October 2003.

14 Henriques Steinberg, "Right Answer, Wrong Score: Test Flaws Take Toll," *New York Times*, May 20, 2001.

15 Ibid.

16 KQED Public Broadcasting, "You Decide: High-Stakes Testing," January 27, 2005, http//:www.kqed.org.

17 "Florida Will Rescore 2006 FCAT Third-Grade Reading Tests," *Orlando Sentinel*, May 24, 2007, http://www.orlandosentinel.com/news/education/orl-bk-fcat05222007,0,4194252.story?coll=orl-home-headlines.

18 Steinberg, "Right Answer, wrong score."

19 Justin Pope, Associated Press, "More Colleges Rethinking SAT," *Denver Post*, March 12, 2006.

20 FairTest, the National Center for Fair and Open Testing, "Schools that Do Not Use SAT or ACT Scores for Admitting Substantial Numbers of Students into Bachelor Degree Programs as of Fall 2007," http://www.fairtest.org/optinit.htm.

21 Emily Pyle, "Test Market," *Texas Observer* (Austin), May 13, 2005.

22 Barbara Miner, "Testing Companies Mine for Gold," *Rethinking Schools*, Winter 2005.

23 Kathy Emery and Susan Ohanion, *Why Is Corporate America Bashing Our Public Schools?* (Portsmouth, NH: Heinemann, 2004).

24 Jennifer Booher-Jennings, "Below the Bubble: 'Educational Triage' and the Texas Accountability System," *American Educational Research Journal* 42, 2 (Summer 2005), 231–268.

25 Jan Fortune-Wood, *Doing It Their Way: Home-based Education and Autonomous Learning* (Nottingham, UK: Educational Heretics Press, 2000), 9.

26 Vermont Society for the Study of Education, *Not the Official DIBELS Clearinghouse*, March 12, 2006, http://vsse.net/dibels.

27 Susan Ohanian, "When Childhood Collides with NCLB" (Brandon: Vermont Society for the Study of Education, 2008).

28 Jeanine Blomberg, Florida Commissioner, "Just Read Florida," New Department of Education, http://www.justreadflorida.com/docs/Read_to_Learn.pdf.

29 Terrence Stutz, "16% Fail TAKS Graduation Test, Record Number Won't Get Diploma: Blacks, Hispanics Hit Hardest," *Dallas Morning News*, May 12, 2007.

30 Theodore Sizer, *Horace's Hope: What Works for the American High School* (New York: Houghton Mifflin, 1997).

31 Lauren Leslie and JoAnne Caldwell, *Qualitative Reading Inventory* (Longman, WA: Addison-Wesley, 1995).

32 Sam Dillon, "School Electives Getting Left Behind," *New York Times*, March 26, 2006.

CHAPTER 2: FROM STANDARDS TO STANDARDIZATION

1 *Merriam-Webster's Collegiate Dictionary*, 10th ed. (Springfield, MA: Merriam-Webster, 1983).

2 Willard Wirtz and Archie Lapointe, *Measuring the Quality of Education: A Report on Assessing Educational Progress* (Washington, DC: Wirtz and Lapointe, 1982), 2.

3 National Commission on Excellence in Education, *A Nation at Risk: A Report to the Nation* (Washington, DC: U.S. Government Printing Office, 1983).

4 Ibid.

5 David C. Berliner and Bruce J. Biddle, *The Manufactured Crisis: Myths, Fraud, and the Attack on America's Public Schools* (New York: Addison-Wesley, 1995).

6 Goals 2000, HR 1804, Educate America Act, as signed into law by President Clinton on March 31, 1994.

7 Alabama State Board of Education, *Alabama Course of Study, Grades 7–12*, Vol. 1, Bulletin No. 7 (Montgomery: Alabama State Board of Education, 1964).

8 Ibid., vii–viii.

9 Nancy Mann, elementary school teacher, conceptualized the wax museum at Rock Ridge Elementary School in 1997. She currently teaches third grade at Flagstone Elementary in Douglas County, Colorado.

10 Roni Jo Draper and Daniel Siebert, "Different Goals, Similar Practices: Making Sense of the Mathematics and Literacy Instruction in a Standards-Based Mathematics Classroom," *American Educational Research Journal* 41, 4 (Winter 2004): 927–962.

11 Science Standards, Douglas County School District Re. 1, adopted December 1996.

12 Alfie Kohn, *The Case Against Standardized Testing: Raising the Scores, Ruining the Schools* (Portsmouth, NH: Heinemann, 2000), 7.

13 Alabama State Board of Education, *Alabama Course of Study*, 3.

14 Alabama Department of Education, adopted 1999, effective for the 2001–2002 school year, available at http://www.alsde.edu/html/home.asp.

15 Boettcher Foundation, Ann Cameron Robb, 3. Accessed at http://www.boettcherfoundation.org/pdf/Boettcher-Times.

16 Alabama High School Graduation Task Force, *Today's Students,*

Tomorrow's Citizens: Pathways for Learning, Language, and Reading Comprehension, Bulletin No. 16 (1997), 57–59.

17 See, for example, E. D. Hirsh, *Cultural Literacy: What Every American Needs to Know* (New York: Houghton Mifflin, 1987), and *The New First Dictionary of Cultural Literacy* (New York: Mariner Books, 2004).

18 Frank Smith, *To Think* (New York : Teachers College, Columbia University, 1991), 27.

19 Benito Mussolini and Giovanni Gentile, *The Doctrine of Fascism* (Rome: Ardita, 1932). Available online at http://www.worldfuturefund. org/wffmaster/Reading/Germany/mussolini.

20 Roderick Stackleberg and Sally Winkle, eds., *The Nazi Germany Sourcebook: An Anthology of Texts,* "Law on the Hitler Youth, 1 December 1936, The Fuhrer and Chancellor of the Reich: Adolf Hitler, the Permanent Secretary and Chief of the Reich Chancellery: Dr. Lammers" (London: Routledge, 2002), article 4, 204–205.

21 Ibid., "Law for the Restoration of the Professional Civil Service, 7 April 1933: The Fuhrer and Chancellor of the Reich: Adolf Hitler, the Reich Minister of the Interior: Frick, the Reich Minister of Finance: Count Schwerin von Krosigk" (London: Routledge, 2002), 150.

22 Lina Haag, "A Handful of Dust," in Stackleberg and Winkle, *The Nazi Germany Sourcebook,* 149.

23 U.S. Supreme Court, *American Communications Association v. Douds* (docket #10), 1950.

CHAPTER 3: ACCOUNTABILITY FEIGNED

1 Kathy Emery and Susan Ohanian, *Why Is Corporate America Bashing Our Public Schools?* (Portsmouth, NH: Heinemann, 2004).

2 Samuel Stringfield and Mary Yakimowski-Srebnick, "Promise, Progress, Problems, and Paradoxes of Three Phases of Accountability: A Longitudinal Case Study of the Baltimore City Public Schools," *American Educational Research Journal* 42, 1 (Spring 2005): 43–75.

3 Emily Pyle, "Test Market: High-Stakes Tests Aren't Good for Teachers, Students, or Schools, So Who Are They Good For?" *Texas Observer* (Austin), May 13, 2005.

4 Center for Responsive Politics, http://www.opensecrets.org.

5 Pyle, "Test Market."

6 The National Conference of State Legislators (NCSL), presentation to the Colorado Legislatures Joint Education Committee, Thursday, February 15, 2007.

7 2004 Investor Fact Book, McGraw-Hill.

8 U.S. House of Representatives; Education and Labor Committee Investigation into the Reading First Program, April 20, 2007.

9 National Center for Education Statistics, "National Evaluation of Early Reading First: Final Report to Congress," May 15, 2007, http://nces.ed.gov/pubsearch/pubsinfo.asp?pubid=NCEE20074007.

10 Claudia Wallis and Sonja Steptoe, "Report Card on No Child Left Behind," *Time*, June 4, 2007, 41.

11 E-mail correspondence from Marion Brady to Senator Kennedy and author, August 15, 2007.

12 David Tyack and Larry Cuban, *Tinkering Toward Utopia: A Century of Public School Reform* (Cambridge, MA: Harvard University Press, 1995), 84.

13 "Trying to Stay Ahead of the Game: Superintendents and Principles Talk About School Leadership," Public Agenda, Reality Check Survey 2001. Available online at http://www.publicagenda.org/reports/trying-stay-ahead-game.

14 Thomas Smith and Richard Ingersoll, "What Are the Effects of Induction and Mentoring on Beginning Teacher Turnover?" *American Educational Research Journal* 41, 3 (Fall 2004): 681–714.

15 Goodwin Liu, National Citizenship and the Promise of Equal Educational Opportunity, *Yale Law Journal Pocket Part* 116 (2006): 145, accessed at http://www.thepocketpart.org/2006/11/21/liu.html.

16 John Cronin, Michael Dahlin, Deborah Adkins, and G. Gage Kingsbury, "The Proficiency Illusion," Thomas B. Fordham Institute, October 4, 2007, http://edexcellence.net/doc/The_Proficiency_Illusion.pdf.

17 Kevin Welner and Alex Molnar, "Truthiness in Education," *Education Week*, February 28, 2007, 2. Results at www.thinktankreview.org.

18 Anthony Pellegrini and Catherine Bohn, "The Role of Recess in Children's Cognitive Performance and School Adjustment," *Educational Researcher* 34, 1, American Educational Research Association (January 2005): 13–19.

19 *Denver Post*, "Let Kids Have Their Recess," editorial, March 18, 2006.

20 Philip Abbott, *Political Thought in America; Conversations and Debates*, 2nd ed. (Prospect Heights, IL: Waveland Press, 1998), 15.

21 Gail Hoagland, National Civic League, *Civic Indicators Handbook*, 2005, 49.

22 Hilda Borko, "Professional Development and Teacher Learning: Mapping the Terrain," *Educational Researcher* 33, 8, American Educational Research Association (November 2004): 3–15.

23 Pamela Grossman and Clarissa Thompson, "District Policy and Beginning Teachers: A Lens on Teacher Learning," *Educational Evaluation and Policy Analysis* 26, 4 (Winter 2004): 281–301.

24 Matt Miller, "State of the Union: First Kill All the School Boards," *Atlantic*, January/February 2008.

25 Karen Seashore Louis, Karen Febey, and Roger Schroeder, "State-Mandated Accountability in High Schools: Teachers' Interpretations of a New Era," *Educational Evaluation and Policy Analysis* 27, 2 (Summer 2005): 177–204.

26 Hoagland, *Civic Indicators Handbook*, 9.

27 Harvey Kantor, "Education, Social Reform, and the State: ESEA and Federal Education Policy in the 1960s," *American Journal of Education* (1991): 47–83.

28 Eric Schaps, "Why the No Child Left Behind Act Is Unsalvageable," *Education Week*, May 8, 2007.

29 Don Perl, personal communication, April 12, 2008. Perl is the founder and president of the Coalition for Better Education, http://www.thecbe.org.

CHAPTER 4: CHALLENGES

1 Chris O'Brien, "How Many H-1B workers? Counts Vary," *San Jose Mercury*, July 15, 2007.

2 Richard Florida, *The Rise of the Creative Class: And How It's Transforming Work, Leisure, Community, and Everyday Life* (New York: Basic Books, 2002), xix.

3 Edison's student achievement has been mixed at best, and its claims about academic improvement never held up to scrutiny. A July 2002 *New York Times* analysis of Edison's claims found that the troubled Cleveland, Ohio, school system achieved higher gains than Edison's schools when analyzed with the methodology Edison applied to its own schools' achievement.

4 See http://pasaorg.tripod.com/edison/edison.html#Lawsuits.

5 John Schwartz, *New York Times*, March 27, 2009, available at http://www.nytimes.com/2009/03/27/us/27judges.html?ref=todayspaper.

6 Edward Liu and Peske Johnson, "New Teachers and the Massachusetts Signing Bonus: The Limits of Inducements," *Educational Evaluation and Policy Analysis* 26, 3 (Fall 2004): 217–236.

7 Dr. Rogier Gregoire, Ed. D., personal communication, March 2008.

8 Mike Rose, *The Mind at Work: Valuing the Intelligence of the American Worker* (New York: Viking, 2004).

9 Jerry Wartgow, *Why School Reform Is Failing and What We Need to Do About It: 10 Lessons from the Trenches* (Lanham, MD: Rowman and Littlefield Education, 2007).

10 Angela Engel, "We're Just Saying No to the CSAP," *Daily Camera* (Boulder, CO), March 18, 2007; Bob Greenlee, "Adults Acting as Children?" *Daily Camera*, April 8, 2007.

11 Rebecca Callahan, "Tracking and High School English Learn-

ers: Limiting Opportunity to Learn," *American Educational Research Journal* 42, 2 (Summer 2005): 305–328.

12 John Robert Warren and Melanie R. Edwards, "High School Exit Examinations and High School Completion: Evidence from the Early 1990's," *Educational Evaluation and Policy Analysis* 27, 1 (Spring 2005): 53–74.

13 Deborah Hicks, "Labor Histories," *Educational Researcher* 34, 3, American Educational Research Association (April 2005): 34.

14 The data presented here are from the Current Population Survey (CPS), 2006 Annual Social and Economic Supplement (ASEC), the source of official poverty estimates. The CPS ASEC is a sample survey of approximately 100,000 households nationwide. These data reflect conditions in calendar year 2005.

15 Erik Eckholm, "Childhood Poverty Is Found to Portend High Adult Costs," *New York Times,* January 25, 2007.

16 Karen Bierman, Head Start REDI, *Child Development Journal,* November/December 2008.

17 http://www2.acf.dhhs.gov/programs/hsb/research/2007.htm, Office of Head Start, 2007 Fact Sheet.

18 http://pubdb3.census.gov/macro/032005/pov/new01_100_01.htm, U.S. Census Bureau, children under 5 below 100 percent poverty; http://nces.ed.gov/programs/coe/list/i4.asp-finance equity; http://www.law.nyu.edu/journals/lawreview/issues/vol81/no6/NYU603.pdf; and http://nces.ed.gov/programs/digest/d05/tables/dt05_094.asp-segregation.

19 http://www.urban.org/url.cfm?ID=901032, Task Force on Poverty of the Center for American Progress, Economic Costs of Child Poverty, January 24, 2007.

20 Jeanne Powers, "High-Stakes Accountability and Equity: Using Evidence from California's Public Schools Accountability Act to Address the Issues in *Williams v. State of California*," *American Educational Research Journal* 41, 4 (Winter 2004), 763–795.

21 Goodwin Liu, "*National Citizenship and the Promise of Equal Educational Opportunity,*" *Yale Law Journal Pocket Part* 116(2006): 145, accessed at http://www.thepocketpart.org/2006/11/21/liu.html.

22 Ibid., 150.

23 Edwin J. Feulner and Doug Wilson, *Getting America Right: The True Conservative Values Our Nation Needs Today* (New York: Crown Forum, 2006), 6.

24 Senator Chuck Schumer, *Positively American: Winning Back the Middle-Class Majority One Family at a Time* (New York: Rodale Books, 2007).

25 Thomas Dee and Jeffry Levine, "The Fate of New Funding: Evidence from Massachusetts' Education Finance Reforms," *Educational Evaluation and Policy Analysis* 26, 3 (Fall 2004): 199–215.

26 Richard Valencia, Angela Valenzuela, Kris Sloan, and Douglas

Foley, "Let's Treat the Cause, Not the Symptoms: Equity and Accountability in Texas Revisited," *Phi Delta Kappan* 83, 4 (Winter 2004): 318–326.

27 Gloria Ladson-Billings, "Landing on the Wrong Note: The Price We Paid for *Brown*," *Educational Researcher* 33, 7, American Educational Research Association (October 2004): 3–13.

28 Liu, "National Citizenship."

29 Harvard University Civil Rights Project, "*Brown* at 50: King's Dream or Plessy's Nightmare," 2004.

30 Jaekyung Lee and Kenneth Wong, "The Impact of Accountability on Racial and Socioeconomic Equity: Considering Both School Resources and Achievement Outcomes," *American Educational Research Journal* 41, 4 (Winter 2004): 797–832.

31 Richard Rothstein, *Class and Schools: Using Social, Economic, and Educational Reform to Close the Black-White Achievement Gap* (New York: Economic Policy Institute, 2004).

32 Mishel Lawrence, Jared Bernsteirn, and Sylvia Allegretto, *The State of Working America. An Economic Policy Institute Book* (Ithaca, NY: ILR Press, an imprint of Cornell University Press, 2005).

33 OECD Program for International Student Assessment, http://www.pisa.oecd.org.

34 Sylvia Allegretto, "Social Expenditures and Child Poverty—the U.S. Is a Noticeable Outlier," *Economic Policy Institute* June 23, 2004.

35 Michael R. Petit, *Homeland Insecurity: American Children at Risk* (Washington, DC: Every Child Matters, 2006), 81.

36 Peter H. Lindert, *Growing Public: Social Spending and Economic Growth Since the Eighteenth Century* (New York: Cambridge University Press, 2004).

37 U.S. Department of Commerce, Bureau of Economic Analysis, "National Income and Product Accounts Table: Table 2.4.5. Personal Consumption Expenditures by Type of Product."Accessed at http://www.bea.gov/bea/dn/nipaweb/TableView.asp?SelectedTable=69&First Year=2002&LastyYear+2005&Freq=Year. Cited in Petit, *Homeland Insecurity,* 43.

CHAPTER 5: CHOICES, CHOICES, CHOICES

1 Standards, Douglas County School District Re. 1, adopted December 1996.

2 Betty Achinstein, Ronald Ogawa, and Anna Speiglman, "Are We Creating Separate and Unequal Tracks of Teachers? The Effects of State Policy, Local Conditions, and Teacher Characteristics on New Teacher Socialization," *American Educational Research Journal* 41, 3 (Fall 2004): 557–603.

3 Jan Fortune-Wood, *Doing It Their Way: Home-based Education and Autonomous Learning* (Nottingham, UK: Educational Heretics Press, 2002), 5.

4 Fortune-Wood, *Doing It Their Way* (citing John Taylor Gatto), 10.

5 Ibid., citing Roland Meighan in a column in *Natural Parenting* 2, December 1997, 13.

6 Lowell Rose and Alec M. Gallup, "The 38th Annual Phi Delta Kappa/Gallup Poll of the Public's Attitudes Toward the Public Schools, *Phi Delta Kappan*, September 2006, 42.

7 Robert G. Brooks and Judith Stein, eds., *Definitive Studies of Magnet Schools: Voices of Public School Choice* (The Woodlands, TX: Magnet Schools of America, 1999).

8 Rick Posner, *Lives of Passion, School of Hope: How One Public School Ignites a Lifelong Love of Learning* (Boulder, CO: Sentient Publications, 2009).

9 Bill of Rights, First Amendment: "Congress shall make no law respecting an establishment of religion, or prohibiting the free exercise thereof; or abridging the freedom of speech, or of the press; or the right of the people peaceably to assemble, and to petition the government for a redress of grievances."

10 Abraham Lincoln, March 9, 1832, in his first political announcement.

11 See Census Bureau, http://www.census.gov/prod/2006pubs/07statab/educ.pdf, table 204, "School Enrollment: 1970 to 2015."

12 Clyde Prestowitz, *Three Billion New Capitalists: The Great Shift of Power to the East* (New York: Basic Books, 2005).

13 Thomas Dee and Jeffry Levine, "The Fate of New Funding: Evidence from Massachusetts' Education Finance Reforms," *Educational Evaluation and Policy Analysis* 26, 3 (Fall 2004): 199–215.

14 Goodwin Liu, "National Citizenship and the Promise of Equal Educational Opportunity," *Yale Law Journal Pocket Part* 116 (2006), accessed at http://www.thepocketpart.org/2006/11/21/liu.html.

CHAPTER 6: SOLUTIONS

1 For example: "Why do they use salt on the roads if it hurts our ecosystems?" "Why do we only have twenty minutes at lunch recess?" "What's in the chicken nuggets in the lunch room?" and "If multiplication is the opposite of division and vice versa, why can't we just learn one of them?"

2 Steven D. Levitt and Stephen J. Dubner, *Freakonomics: A Rogue Economist Explores the Hidden Side of Everything* (New York: Morrow, 2005).

3 Collins is an educator who in 1975 started Westside Preparatory School in Garfield Park, an impoverished neighborhood of Chicago, Illinois. http://www.marvacollins.com/biography.html.

4 Meiers is often considered the founder of the modern small schools movement. http://www.deborahmeier.com.

5 Sudbury Valley School, http://www.sudval.org; Cristo Rey, http://www.cristoreynetwork.org; the MET, http://www.the metschool.org; and Essential Schools, http://essentialschools.org/publ/ces_docs/ssp/ssp.

6 http://www.acsd1.k12.co.us.

7 Carl Chew, http://www.curewashington.org/carlchewhome; and Don Perl, http://www.thecbe.org.

8 Thomas Jefferson to William C. Jarvis, 1820, available at http://etext.virginia.edu/jefferson/quotations.

9 Steven Wolk, "Why Go to School?" *Phi Delta Kappa,* May 2007, 650.

Index

About the Author

Angela Engel writes from her experiences as a teacher, parent, school administrator, speaker, and policy advisor. Currently a facilitator for the Family Leadership Training Institute, she earned her master's degree in curriculum and instruction from the University of Colorado–Denver. Her work with state legislators has led to policies that improve learning and opportunities for Colorado 's children.

Deborah W. Meier is currently on the faculty of New York University's Steinhardt School of Education, as senior scholar and adjunct professor as well as Board Member and Director of New Ventures at Mission Hill, Director and Advisor to Forum for Democracy and Education, and on the board of the Coalition of Essential Schools.